EDWARD GRANVILLE BROWNE

and

THE BAHÁ'Í FAITH

The author

H. M. Balyuzi came from a Persian family distinguished for its scholarship and administrative ability. His father, a close correspondent of E. G. Browne, was Governor of the Persian Gulf Ports. Although related to the Báb, the Herald and Martyr-Prophet of the New Dispensation, Mr Balyuzi's membership of the Bahá'í Faith is by conviction and not inheritance. He graduated from the American University of Beirut and later took his M.Sc. (Econ) at London. At the outbreak of war in 1939 he joined the Persian service of the BBC. He was, for many years, chairman of the National Spiritual Assembly of the Bahá'ís of the British Isles. He was appointed a Hand of the Cause in 1957, has served in Haifa at the World Centre of the Bahá'í Faith, and travelled, in 1961, through Canada and down to Ecuador and Peru. He died in 1980.

By the same author

Bahá'u'lláh, the King of Glory (a full biography)
Bahá'u'lláh, the Word Made Flesh (a brief life and essay)
The Báb, The Herald of the Day of Days
'Abdu'l-Bahá, The Centre of the Covenant of Bahá'u'lláh
Muhammad and the Course of Islam
Eminent Bahá'ís in the time of Bahá'u'lláh

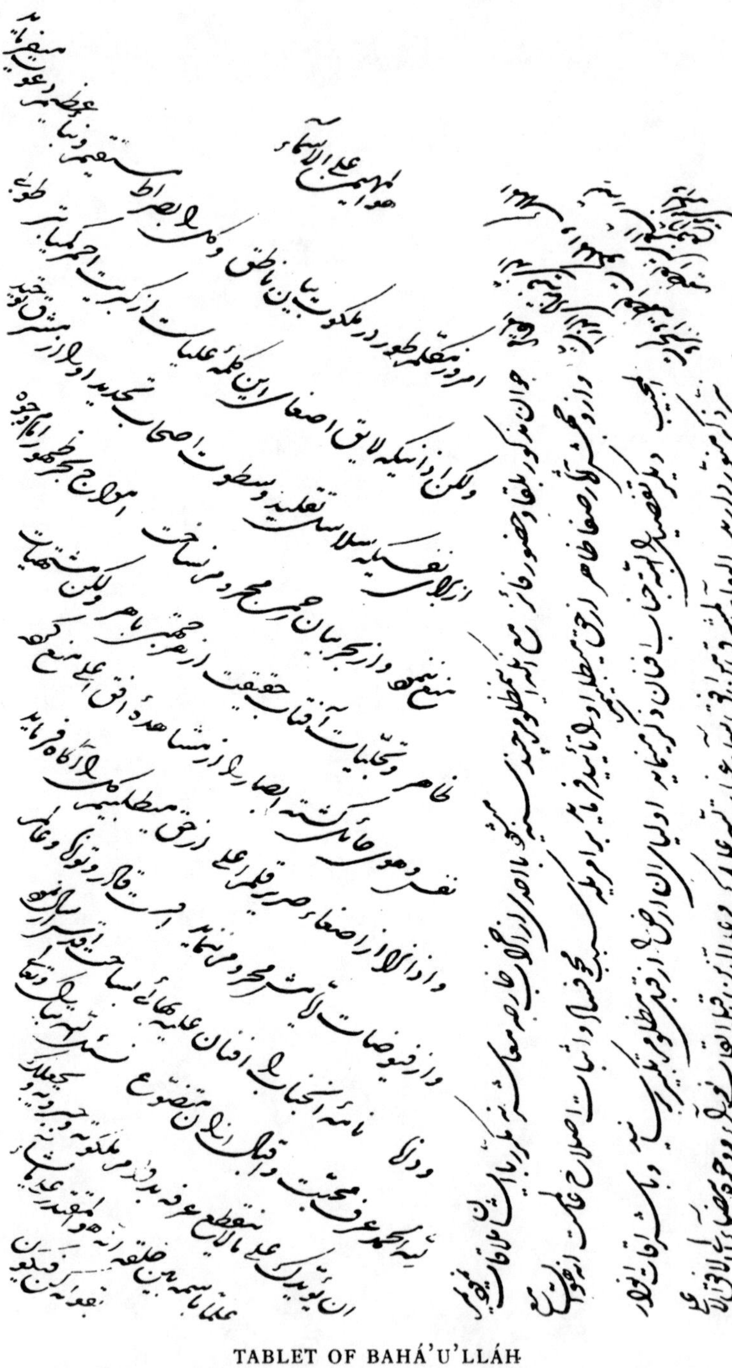

TABLET OF BAHÁ'U'LLÁH

Addressed to the father of the author

Edward Granville BROWNE and THE BAHÁ'Í FAITH

by

H. M. BALYUZI

GEORGE RONALD

OXFORD

First hardcover edition 1970
Reprinted 1975, 1980

ISBN-10: 0–85398–496–4
ISBN-13: 978–0–85398–496–2

*A catalogue record for this book is available
from the British Library*

Acknowledgements

The author wishes to express to the Cambridge University Press sincere gratitude for their kind permission to quote from five published works by Edward Granville Browne which bear upon the theme of this book: *A Year Amongst the Persians*, *A Traveller's Narrative*, *Táríkh-i-Jadíd or New History of the Báb*, *The Persian Revolution of 1905–1909*, and *Materials for the Study of the Bábí Religion*. He feels especially indebted to the Hon. Sir Patrick Browne and Mr Michael Browne for their generous consent to his use of this essential material, and for their permission to quote from letters addressed by Edward Browne to 'Abdu'l-Bahá and to the author's father.

Acknowledgement is also made in warmest terms to the Gibb Memorial Trust for permission to quote from *Kitáb-i-Nuqṭatu'l-Káf*; to the Royal Asiatic Society for the use of extracts from articles by Edward Browne published in their Journal in the years 1889, 1892, and 1922; to Messrs Faber and Faber for the right to reprint four short quotations from *Both Ends of the Candle* by Sir Denison Ross; to Messrs William Heinemann for a brief extract from *An Indian Diary* by Edwin Montagu; to G. P. Putnam's Sons, New York, for some lines from *Abbas Effendi, His Life and Teachings* by Myron Phelps; to the National Spiritual Assembly of the Bahá'ís of the United States for kindly permitting the quotation of passages from *Epistle to the Son of the Wolf* by Bahá'u'lláh, *God Passes By* by Shoghi Effendi, and *Bahá'í World*, vol. IV; and to the Bahá'í Publishing Trust, London, for the use of quotations from their editions of *Gleanings from the Writings of Bahá'u'lláh* and the *Kitáb-i-Íqán* by Bahá'u'lláh, *The Dispensation of Bahá'u'lláh* by Shoghi Effendi, and *The Bahá'í Revelation*, a compilation of Bahá'í Scripture.

Full details of the works mentioned are given in the bibliography. Quotations are reproduced in their original form, even though differing from the spelling and transliteration of Persian words adopted in this book; except that extracts from Bahá'í Scripture are not italicized. Translations from Persian sources are by the author unless otherwise attributed.

Sincere thanks go also to Mr Farhang Jahanpur of Pembroke College, Lector in Persian at Cambridge University, for his assistance in obtaining material included in the collection of Professor Browne's papers in the University Library at Cambridge; and to Mr Horst W. Kolodziej for the care he has taken in photographing original documents reproduced in this book. Finally, to those who have assisted in reading the proofs—Mr R. H. Backwell, Mr Farhang Jahanpur, and Mr Rustom Sabit—the author makes his grateful salute.

Contents

My abiding gratitude is due to Marion and David Hofman for their constant encouragement and invaluable suggestions, and to Abu'l-Qásim Afnán for his very generous aid in my research.

Introduction

On May 22nd 1844, Siyyid 'Alí-Muḥammad, a young merchant of Shíráz, declared to a seeker, Mullá Ḥusayn of Bushrúyih,[1] that He was the Qá'im Whose advent the world of Islám awaited. History knows Him as the Báb—'The Gate'. His claim, amply attested by His Writings, put Him in the same rank as the Manifestations of God preceding Him: Muḥammad, Jesus, Moses, Zoroaster, Buddha, Krishna. His Ministry lasted six years, three of which found Him in prison. He was incarcerated first in the fortress of Máh-kú and later in the fortress of Chihríq, both situated in the Persian province of Ádharbáyján. On July 9th 1850 the Báb was shot in the public square of Tabríz. He was in His thirty-first year. In His lifetime those who had given Him their allegiance were subjected to fierce persecution. Most of His early disciples and hundreds more perished in the holocaust. Two years after His own martyrdom, fresh storms broke over the heads of His followers. Two Bábís, very young in years, frenzied by the sufferings that had befallen their fellow-believers, made a futile and ill-prepared attempt to assassinate the Sháh. They failed and paid the penalty for their deed, and their community, although innocent, stood condemned in the eyes of all. A reign of terror ensued.

Two brothers of noble descent, sons of a late minister[2] of the Crown, were well marked and highly esteemed in the ranks of the Bábís. In that August 1852 when the incredible attempt was made on the life of Náṣiri'd-Dín Sháh (1848–96), the elder Brother, Mírzá Ḥusayn-'Alí, surnamed Bahá'u'lláh (The Glory of God), was staying with friends in a summer resort in the vicinity of Ṭihrán. As soon as the news reached Him, in spite of the pleadings of His hosts who feared for His life, He rode fearlessly towards the Sháh's camp at Níyávarán. A half-brother, thirteen years younger, named Mírzá Yaḥyá, and entitled Ṣubḥ-i-Azal (The Morn of Eternity), who was 'the nominee of the Báb, and recognized chief of the Bábí com-

[1] A small town in the province of Khurásán.
[2] Mírzá Buzurg-i-Núrí.

munity',[1] put on a garb of disguise and went roaming over the countryside.

Bahá'u'lláh was promptly arrested. Under the scorching sun of August He was led into Ṭihrán from the Sháh's camp, a distance of many miles, on foot, in chains, His head and feet bared. The mob, lining the streets, howled and jeered and hurled insults. In Ṭihrán, He was thrown into a dungeon which was called Síyáh-Chál—'The Dark Pit'. There He remained and suffered intolerably for four months, and there, according to His own testimony, He became aware of His Divine mission.

The main theme of the Báb's message had been the advent of One greater than Himself to Whom He referred as 'He Whom God shall make manifest'. His command to His followers to recognise and accept that next Manifestation of God was most emphatic and unequivocal.

In the murk of the dungeon of Ṭihrán Bahá'u'lláh saw the supernal Light heralded by the Báb dawn in His own Person. And there He made a vow. In His own words:

> Day and night, while confined in that dungeon, We meditated upon the deeds, the condition, and the conduct of the Bábís, wondering what could have led a people so high-minded, so noble, and of such intelligence, to perpetrate such an audacious and outrageous act against the person of His Majesty. This Wronged One, thereupon, decided to arise, after His release from prison, and undertake, with the utmost vigor, the task of regenerating this people.[2]

His innocence proved, Bahá'u'lláh was released from prison and with His family was banished from Írán to 'Iráq. The journey in the heart of a severe winter over snow-clad mountains was fraught with immense hardship. Bahá'u'lláh's health, already severely strained, was further impaired. But as soon as He regained His strength He set out to fulfil His vow. Mírzá Yaḥyá, Ṣubḥ-i-Azal, had also, in the meantime, arrived at Baghdád. He had shown no competence, and yet he chose to obstruct the regenerative effort of his Brother. Ere

[1] Shoghi Effendi (Guardian of the Bahá'í Faith), *God Passes By* (Wilmette, 1965), p. 163.

[2] Bahá'u'lláh, *Epistle to the Son of the Wolf* (Wilmette, 1941), p. 21.

long he was deep in intrigue. His conduct forced Bahá'u'lláh to withdraw to the mountains of northern 'Iráq. During His absence it became apparent that Mírzá Yaḥyá was inept and could not preside over the affairs of the Bábí community.

The future looked grim until the Bábís in Baghdád received tidings of Bahá'u'lláh and sent emissaries to ask Him to come back. When Bahá'u'lláh returned after an absence of nearly two years Mírzá Yaḥyá was outwardly silenced, and the Bábí community was in a parlous condition. As Bahá'u'lláh went on openly with the task He had pledged Himself to accomplish, Mírzá Yaḥyá chose to shut himself away, and went under the name of Ḥájí 'Alíy-i-Lásh-Furúsh (The Silk-Dealer). He panicked at any sign of peril. Once he fled to Baṣrah, masquerading as a Jew from Baghdád, trading in shoes.

The rising fame of Bahá'u'lláh alarmed the divines. They took counsel together and urged action upon the ministers of Náṣiri'd-Dín Sháh. These in turn brought pressure upon the Ottoman Government, and Bahá'u'lláh was called to Constantinople. On April 22nd 1863, prior to His departure, Bahá'u'lláh declared to a group of Bábís gathered around Him that He was, in fact, 'He Whom God shall make manifest', proclaimed and promised by the Báb. No dissent is recorded.

Mírzá Yaḥyá obtained a passport under an assumed name, and wended his way to Mosul, where he attached himself to Bahá'u'lláh's entourage and journeyed to the Ottoman capital. From there he went in his Brother's company to Adrianople. Closely associated with him was Siyyid Muḥammad-i-Iṣfahání, who has been called 'the Antichrist of the Bahá'í Revelation', the same man who, in earlier years in Baghdád, had incited Mírzá Yaḥyá to mischief. In the hands of Siyyid Muḥammad, Mírzá Yaḥyá became a malleable tool. 'The nominee of the Báb' became the instrument of denial. He used every means to malign and disparage and injure, even to destroy the Brother Who had reared him, watched over him with tender care, and had at all times tried to protect him from his own follies and from the machinations of the world around him.

The almost universal acceptance by the Bábís of Bahá'u'lláh as 'He Whom God shall make manifest', promised to them by their Martyr-Prophet, drove Mírzá Yaḥyá to desperation. He had failed to find adequate support among the Bábís. Jealousy, dismay, frustration, ambition combined to produce a diabolic plot. Twice, Mírzá Yaḥyá resorted to poison. Bahá'u'lláh bore the mark of it throughout His life. Thwarted, Mírzá Yaḥyá became alarmed. He accused Bahá'u'lláh of trying to poison him and partaking of the poisoned food by mistake.

Next Mírzá Yaḥyá tried to win over to his side the man who served as the barber and the bath attendant of Bahá'u'lláh, and incited him to murder. Ustád Muḥammad-'Alí, the barber, was thunderstruck and livid with rage. Later that day he related the miserable story to 'Abdu'l-Bahá, the eldest Son of Bahá'u'lláh. He has recorded the episode in a written account of his life:

> When the bath-time was over, I went to the Master[1] and said, 'To-day Mírzá Yaḥyá spoke thus to me; I was infuriated and wanted to kill him, but withheld myself'. The Master replied, 'This was a situation which you came to understand. Don't mention it to anyone. It had better remain undisclosed'.

Mírzá Yaḥyá took many a devious and dubious path until he dared not face Bahá'u'lláh in public, even when challenged. Separation became inevitable. Rejected by the community of the Báb, save for a small number, Mírzá Yaḥyá turned to the authorities of the Ottoman Empire in a bid to arouse their wrath. The Persian ambassador in Constantinople[2] was equally active in bringing charges against Bahá'u'lláh. Mírzá Yaḥyá and his partisans sent repeated appeals and complaints to the Sublime Porte.[3] They alleged that Bahá'u'lláh had deprived them of their means of subsistence, and asked for money. Finally they accused Bahá'u'lláh of harbouring thoughts of rebellion, even more, of having a plan actively in hand.

Mírzá Yaḥyá succeeded in his efforts, but he also engulfed himself. When the decree of Sulṭán 'Abdu'l-'Azíz came, inflicting yet another exile on Bahá'u'lláh, Mírzá Yaḥyá, too, was included in the imperial pronouncement. He was sent to Cyprus. There he died in 1912, a bitter, broken man.

[1] 'Abdu'l-Bahá.

[2] Ḥájí Mírzá Ḥusayn Khán, the Mushíru'd-Dawlih, and the Sipahsálár.

[3] Báb-i-'Álí, or the Sublime Porte, indicated the seat of Ottoman power. Hence came the use of this term as a synonym for the Turkish Government.

Bahá'u'lláh with His family and His people reached the citadel of 'Akká where they were to be incarcerated, on August 31st 1868. 'Akká (Acre) was unhealthy, prison conditions were extremely harsh, wardens brutal, townsmen suspicious and hostile. Bahá'u'lláh lost a son in that prison. After two years of great hardship some relief was obtained because the citadel was required for the stationing of troops. Prisoners were let out, but forbidden exit from the city. Seven more years passed before Bahá'u'lláh took residence outside the city walls. Rules laid down by the Sulṭán had not been relaxed. But governors and magistrates, both lay and clerical, were loth to enforce the imperial edict. Indeed they went further. The Muftí of 'Akká pleaded with Bahá'u'lláh to leave the town. The Governor made it known that Bahá'u'lláh would not be hindered should He wish to live in the country. The inhabitants of 'Akká, except for a few die-hards, were no longer antagonistic, and many of them had become friendly. The transformation, although gradual, was almost complete. It had been effected chiefly by the grace and courtesy and charm and patience of 'Abbás Effendi, the Son of Bahá'u'lláh, Who adopted 'Abdu'l-Bahá (Servant of Bahá) as His designation, when He succeeded His Father. Midḥat Pá<u>sh</u>á, the celebrated Ottoman statesman whom the Turks have revered as 'the Father of the Constitution', hearing of the renown of the Son of Bahá'u'lláh, invited Him to visit Beirut. There <u>Sh</u>ay<u>kh</u> Muḥammad 'Abduh, the future Grand Muftí of Egypt, hailed throughout the Islamic world as one of its most remarkable figures in modern times, met 'Abdu'l-Bahá and became a fervent admirer.[1]

Bahá'ís, long denied access to the presence of Bahá'u'lláh, could come and go in increasing numbers, unmolested. The closing years of the life of Bahá'u'lláh were spent in the tranquil surroundings of the Mansion of Bahjí. Situated within three miles of the city-walls, Bahjí was called a 'palace'—a building of majestic proportions commanding the vast plain. During the darkest days of His incarceration Bahá'u'lláh had foretold that one day He would pitch His tent on Mount Carmel, and that came to pass.

The only Westerner of note who witnessed this amazing change of fortune was Edward Granville Browne of Pembroke College,

[1] This meeting took place in 1878.

Cambridge, then at the outset of his distinguished career. He visited Bahá'u'lláh in April 1890, two years prior to His ascension.[1]

The name of E. G. Browne stands very high among orientalists of this or any age. His fame is supported by solid, enduring achievement. But in the works of this renowned scholar Mírzá Yaḥyá is given a prominence which is misleading. It has actually misled some whose sincerity is above reproach, and has also provided argument to men obviously hostile to the Faith of Bahá'u'lláh. That Professor Edward Browne deeply and sincerely felt the power of Bahá'u'lláh and 'Abdu'l-Bahá when he came face to face with Them, that he paid moving and eloquent tributes to that power, that his writings served to bring the Bahá'í Faith to the notice of Western scholars, are indubitable facts which no Bahá'í can or would wish to ignore or deny. That which is due to Edward Granville Browne must be gratefully recognised. But it is also a fact that Edward Browne was tragically mistaken, that his considerable prestige aided the furtherance of the designs of the adversaries of the Faith of Bahá'u'lláh.

The present writer feels qualified to explore this theme. His father knew Edward Browne intimately in London in the eighties of the last century, was featured as Mírzá 'Alí in Browne's *A Year Amongst the Persians*, corresponded with him for some years, and more significant, he was instrumental in facilitating Browne's visit to 'Akká and to Bahá'u'lláh.

It cannot be left unsaid that regrettably a host of writers, whenever they have had occasion to refer to the Faith of the Báb and Bahá'u'lláh, have not taken sufficient care to sift fact from fiction. In some instances, seemingly, one author has simply perpetuated a myth given currency by a predecessor. As far as the present writer recalls he has seldom come across a press account of any event of which he has had close personal knowledge without detecting either plain error or inadequate reporting. What one finds in the press one ought not to find in the considered works of authors of justifiably

[1] May 29th 1892.

high repute. It is strange to see Mr H. Kamshad presenting Bahá'u'lláh and Ṣubḥ-i-Azal as 'descendants' of the Báb, and 'Abdu'l-Bahá as the 'founder of Bahaism'.[1] Also strange is Mr Peter Avery's statement that Bahá'u'lláh was the 'chosen successor' to the Báb.[2] Stranger is Mme Věra Kubíčková's reference to Ḥájí Mírzá Yaḥyá Dawlatábádí as a member of 'the Bahā'ī sect'[3]—a proficient man-of-letters and a famous politician, who was in no way favourably inclined towards the Bahá'í Faith. Prof. Joseph M. Upton states that it was Ṣubḥ-i-Azal who was 'transferred to Adrianople at the request of the Shah'.[4] Mr John Marlowe in a footnote asserts that 'Bahai'ism is a heretical variant of Islam'.[5] Mr Donald N. Wilber mentions that some 40,000 Bábís were massacred about two years after the martyrdom of the Báb, and that Mírzá Yaḥyá 'settled at Adrianople'.[6] These are only a few instances chosen at random from more recent works.

It is hoped that this monograph will help to redress the balance.

[1] H. Kamshad, *Modern Persian Prose Literature* (Cambridge, 1966), p. 51.

[2] P. Avery, *Modern Iran* (London, 1965), p. 65.

[3] J. Rypka, *History of Iranian Literature* (Dordrecht, 1968), p. 374. (See bibliography for further details.)

[4] J. M. Upton, *The History of Modern Iran, An Interpretation*, Harvard Middle Eastern Monographs II (Cambridge, Massachausetts, 1960), p. 10.

[5] J. Marlowe, *Iran (A Short Political Guide)* (London and Dunmow, 1963), p. 9.

[6] D. N. Wilber, *Iran, Past and Present* (Princeton, New Jersey, 1967), p. 77.

Chapter I

Edward Browne—Early Years

In his Introduction to his celebrated book, *A Year Amongst the Persians*,[1] Edward Browne writes,

> It was the Turkish war with Russia in 1877–8 that first attracted my attention to the East, about which, till that time, I had known and cared nothing... At first my proclivities were by no means for the Turks; but the losing side, more especially when it continues to struggle gallantly against defeat, always has a claim on our sympathy, and moreover the cant of the anti-Turkish party in England, and the wretched attempts to confound questions of abstract justice with party politics, disgusted me beyond measure. Ere the close of the war I would have died to save Turkey, and I mourned the fall of Plevna as though it had been a disaster inflicted on my own country. And so gradually pity turned to admiration, and admiration to enthusiasm, until the Turks became in my eyes veritable heroes, and the desire to identify myself with their cause, make my dwelling amongst them, and unite with them in the defence of their land, possessed me heart and soul.

Thus began the pull of the East for the young Edward Browne who was then no more than sixteen years old.

Edward Granville Browne was born at Uley in Gloucestershire on February 7th 1862. His father, Sir Benjamin Browne, was a noted industrialist of Newcastle-on-Tyne. There was nothing in the background of his family, which sprang from Gloucestershire, to presage his brilliant academic career and the intense love for Persia which was to characterize his life. His school days at Glenalmond and Eton were not happy days for him. But at Pembroke College, Cambridge, he found a congenial home as a student, and in later years as a Fellow, Lecturer and Professor. Sir Benjamin wished his son to follow in his footsteps and study engineering. However, medicine proved more attractive to young Edward. And at Cambridge he found

[1] E. G. Browne, *A Year Amongst the Persians* (Cambridge, 1926), p. 8.

opportunities to study Turkish. Exaggerated nationalism has, for good or ill, changed the face of Turkish in this century. Great writers of Turkish prose and poetry who flourished in the decades preceding the first world war[1] would find themselves in the wilderness today. But in the eighties of the nineteenth century Turkish had far more recognisable relationships with Persian and Arabic. Thus it was that Edward Browne went on from Turkish to study the other two languages.

In the summer of 1882, three years after his admission to Cambridge, Edward Browne spent two months in Istanbul. That was his first experience of the East. Back in Cambridge, he pursued with added vigour his study of Persian. He took lessons from a learned Indian. Then whilst continuing his medical studies in London at St Bartholomew's Hospital, he came, in the year 1884, to meet a number of Persians, one of whom was the writer's father, also a student in London. But the most remarkable Persian whom Browne met, and from whom he received tuition in the language of his quest, was a man, in Browne's own words: 'very learned but very eccentric'. Mírzá Muḥammad-Báqir of the town of Bavánát in the province of Fárs, who had gained the notorious appellation of 'Káfir' (The Infidel) was a man who had roamed the world, acquiring languages and fresh names, and adopting a variety of religious beliefs. In turn he had been a Muslim, a Christian (calling himself John), a Jew (then taking on the name, Ibráhím),[2] an atheist, and at the time he met Browne his primary concern was to promulgate a religious system of his own making. To that end he had written a great deal (in English as well) including a tediously long and weird poem entitled *Shumaysiy-i-Landaníyyih* or *The Little Sun of London.*[3] This poem laden with strangest words, notions, imagery and phraseology, he forced his pupil diligently to learn. His daughter was seriously ill, and physicians had advised moving to a warmer climate, as a matter of urgency. But he would not leave Limehouse until Browne had mastered the whole of the 366 verses of his 'Sunlet', departing with his ailing daughter the following day.

[1] Such as Shinásí Effendi and Kimál Bey. [2] Abraham.

[3] W. H. Allen and Co., and R. J. Mitchell and Sons (London, 1882). His poetical soubriquet was Mu'aṭṭar (Fragrant).

Edward Browne learned Persian exceedingly well. His command of the language was truly outstanding. However, his medical studies occupied him until the year 1887.

How and when did Browne come to know of the Faith of the Báb and Bahá'u'lláh? Writing in 1891 his Introduction to the translation which he made of *A Traveller's Narrative*,[1] he related the story of his first encounter with this Faith:

> One day some seven years ago I was searching amongst the books in the University Library of Cambridge for fresh materials for an essay on the Ṣúfí philosophy, in the study of which I was then chiefly engaged, when my eye was caught by the title of Count Gobineau's *Religions et Philosophies dans l'Asie Centrale*. I took down the book, glanced through it to discover whether or no it contained any account of the Ṣúfís, and, finding that a short chapter was devoted to them, brought it back with me to my rooms. My first superficial glance had also shewn me that a considerable portion of the book was taken up with an account of the Bábís, of which sect I had at that time no definite knowledge, save a general idea that they had been subjected to a most severe persecution.[2]

For Browne, Gobineau's treatment of the Ṣúfí doctrine was disappointing:

> When, however, I turned from this mournful chapter to that portion of the book which treated of the Bábí movement, the case was altogether different. To anyone who has already read this masterpiece of historical composition, this most perfect presentation of accurate and critical research in the form of a narrative of thrilling and sustained interest, such as one may, indeed, hope to find in the drama or the romance, but can scarcely expect from the historian, it is needless to describe the effect which it produced on me. . . I had long ardently desired to visit Persia and above all Shíráz, and this desire was now greatly intensified. But whereas I

[1] A manuscript copy in the handwriting of an eminent Bahá'í, Zaynu'l-Muqarrabín, was given to Browne in Bahjí, 'Akká, in 1890. This book was written by 'Abdu'l-Bahá, but at that time its authorship was anonymous. Browne had that manuscript published in facsimile (vol. I of *A Traveller's Narrative*, see bibliography).

[2] E. G. Browne (ed.), *A Traveller's Narrative written to illustrate The Episode of the Báb* (Cambridge, 1891), vol. II, ix–x.

had previously wished to see Shíráz because it was the home of Ḥáfiẓ and of Sa'dí, I now wished to see it because it was the birthplace of Mírzá 'Alí Muḥammad the Báb.[1]

However it was not until 1887 when Edward Browne had just concluded his medical studies, and had unexpectedly been elected a Fellow of his College (Pembroke) at Cambridge, that the long-sought opportunity to visit Persia came his way.

Browne crossed the Turkish frontier into Persia, heading for Tabríz,[2] on October 23rd 1887. On September 27th 1888, homeward bound, he boarded a Russian steamer at Mashhad-i-Sar (now named Bábulsar) on the Caspian Sea. This sojourn on Persian soil became the subject of a work brilliantly written, to which he gave the title, *A Year Amongst the Persians*. It was published in 1893 by Messrs A. and C. Black. Page after page of this delightful book, which undoubtedly has an honoured place in the ranks of world classics, is devoted to the people whom Edward Browne calls the 'Bábís', although by that year of 1888, all of them, except a very small number, had long before taken the appellation 'Bahá'í'.

Browne was very eager from the day that he set foot in Persia to find the followers of the new Faith, but in a land where their very name was anathema, the search of the young Englishman seemed foredoomed to failure. Four months had gone and Edward Browne had reached Iṣfahán when one day 'a vendor of curiosities' whispered into his ears that he was one of the very people whom the Englishman was seeking. What made this Bahá'í of Iṣfahán take a course so precipitate Browne himself was at a loss to explain. This was only the unexpected beginning of a vast and varied adventure.

In Iṣfahán Browne met for an hour or two one of the most remarkable Bahá'ís of all times, Ḥájí Mírzá Ḥaydar-'Alí, who had known nine years of banishment in Khartoum,[3] first in chains and close confinement and later in relative freedom (during the governorship of Ismá'íl Páshá Ayyúb), until released by the arrival of General Gordon in 1877. However it was in Shíráz, the birthplace of the glorious Báb Himself, to which city Edward Browne proceeded

[1] *ibid.*, x–xi.
[2] It was in this town in northwest Persia that the Báb was shot on July 9th 1850.
[3] Then newly built in the Súdán.

from Iṣfahán, that he first had the opportunity of intimate and long talks with the Bahá'ís. There he met once again the friend[1] whom he had known in London in his student days, who was related to the Báb, and through whom Browne was introduced to other members of His family. Later, in the city of Yazd, Browne made the acquaintance of still more members of the family[2] of the Báb. Not a single one of them did he find to have pledged his allegiance to Mírzá Yaḥyá, Ṣubḥ-i-Azal. They were one and all followers of Bahá'u'lláh. Three years later when he had achieved his object of visiting Bahá'u'lláh, in the Mansion of Bahjí, 'Akká, Browne met, in his own words 'a very old man with light blue eyes and white beard, whose green turban proclaimed him a descendant of the Prophet'. He goes on to say,

> When I discovered that this venerable old man was not only one of the original companions of the Báb but his relative and comrade from earliest childhood, it may well be imagined with what eagerness I gazed upon him and listened to his every utterance.[3]

This 'venerable old man' was a brother of the wife of the Báb and His cousin.[4]

It was the power and the argument of the *Kitáb-i-Íqán* (The Book of Certitude) revealed by Bahá'u'lláh during the Baghdád period, for a maternal uncle[5] of the Báb, which convinced that uncle of the truth of his Nephew's mission. Indeed apart from His wife and one other maternal uncle[6]—who reared the Báb when His father's death left Him unprotected, and who eventually died[7] for His Cause—none of the relatives of the Báb embraced the Faith of which He was the Bearer until later years, and then under the aegis of Bahá'u'lláh.

The present writer has in his possession a diary for the year 1888, kept by his father, which records Edward Browne's visit to Shíráz. He also possesses letters written to his father by Browne, upon his return to England. Of these more will be said later.

[1] The father of the present writer.

[2] Bahá'u'lláh gave to this family and its members the designation, Afnán (Twigs).

[3] Browne (ed.), *A Traveller's Narrative*, vol. II, xxxvii–xxxviii.

[4] Ḥájí Mírzá Siyyid Ḥasan, known as Afnán-i-Kabír (The Great Afnán), a great-grandfather of the present writer.

[5] Ḥájí Siyyid Muḥammad. [6] Ḥájí Mírzá Siyyid 'Alí.

[7] He was one of the Seven Martyrs of Ṭihrán, put to death in March 1850.

From Shíráz Browne went to Yazd where he was well received by the relatives of the Báb; and from Yazd he went to Kirmán. It was there that he met Azalís for the first time. A connection was thus established between the young, eager orientalist and that small number of Bábís who for various reasons looked to Mírzá Yaḥyá as their guide and mentor. It was a connection that was destined to have unforeseen consequences. It also happened that Kirmán contained a number of Bahá'ís whose behaviour was erratic and strange. Apart from these Azalís and Bahá'ís, Edward Browne was surrounded in Kirmán by an ill-assorted group of people harbouring diverse fantasies. He has himself recorded that there he was led to smoke opium, and nearly became an addict.[1] This city, the company of its inhabitants, and its associations held him almost spellbound. He wrote:

> I . . . found myself ere long in a world whereof I had never dreamed, and wherein my spirit was subjected to such alternations of admiration, disgust, and wonder, as I had never before in my life experienced.[2]

By October 10th 1888, Edward Browne was back in England, a Fellow of Pembroke College and Reader in Persian at the University of Cambridge. On his return journey, he had once again visited Ṭihrán, this time being well provided with introductions to some of the Bahá'ís of the capital. Of them he writes, 'They entertained me at lunch . . . and I was much impressed by their piety and gravity of

[1] Sir Denison Ross (1871–1940), scholar, orientalist, and the first Director of the School of African and Oriental Studies in London, has this reference in his autobiography, *Both Ends of the Candle* (London, 1943), to Edward Browne's encounter with opiates: 'Before I went to India [1901], besides constantly running down to Pembroke, I spent several long vacations there. In those days there was very delightful company at the High Table, and after dinner in the Combination Room. . . From the Combination Room we used to move to Browne's rooms, where we were always joined by a number of undergraduates. On one of these evenings we tried table-turning, and I remember being raced down the funny old staircase into the quad by the little round table I was practising on with Jack Atkins. On another occasion E. G. B. produced some hashish he had brought from Persia (he had nearly fallen a victim to the drug there), and several of us tried it, including myself. It produced the most extraordinary sensations of happiness and exaggeration. Everything in the room seemed to grow to immense proportions, one losing all sense of one's size.' (p. 55)

[2] Browne, *A Year Amongst the Persians*, p. 476.

demeanour, so unlike the anarchic freedom of the Kirmán Bábís.'[1]

Browne settled down soon to work on the Bábí and Bahá'í manuscripts which he had obtained in Persia, and on the copious notes which he had taken. The immediate result of his researches was two papers which appeared in the *Journal of the Royal Asiatic Society*, the first in the July issue of 1889, and the second in the October issue of the same year. In a letter dated April 9th 1889 to the father of the present writer Browne mentions their forthcoming publication:

> I have been elected lately to the Royal Asiatic Society, and they asked me to read a paper there on Monday next which I have been very busy preparing—It is to be on the Bábís—The first paper will be about their history and present state: the second (to be read on June 17th) on their doctrines and literature. The papers will probably be printed in the autumn, and I shall of course send you copies—

Thanking his correspondent at the start for 'your delightful letter dated Jan. 3rd of this year', Browne mentions having received with that letter 'a copy made by your uncle, Áḳá Mírzá Seyyid Huseyn[2] [sic], of the *Lawḥ-i-Malika*[3] [sic], for which I am extremely grateful'. He goes on to say, 'I have written a few lines to thank him, which I enclose in this letter, and which I trust you will present to him with my selâms[4] [sic] and sincere thanks.' This was a copy of the Tablet which Bahá'u'lláh had addressed to Queen Victoria.

In the same letter Browne writes:

> I have been examining some Bábí M.S.S. in the British Museum, and find they have one of the *Persian Beyán*[5] [sic], (the same which I obtained in Persia), which corresponds with mine in length so that I have no doubt it is the complete work. This copy was written by *Nabíl*, and is well written in Naskh,[6] while mine is in *Shikasta*[7] [sic]—On looking through my copy of Alwáḥ,[8] I find that that of the French Emperor[9] is not included, for this I am

[1] Browne, *A Year Amongst the Persians*, p. 601.

[2] Áqá Siyyid Muḥammad-Ḥusayn, a nephew of the wife of the Báb, and the paternal grandfather of Shoghi Effendi, Guardian of the Bahá'í Faith.

[3] *Lawḥ-i-Malikih* (Tablet to the Queen).

[4] Saláms (Salutations).

[5] *Bayán*, a major Writing of the Báb.

[6] A style of calligraphy.

[7] Shikastih, another style of handwriting, developed by the Persians.

[8] Tablets of Bahá'u'lláh.

[9] Napoleon III.

very sorry. If you could at any time get me a copy of that, and of the *Lawḥ-i-Sheykh Báḳir*[1] [sic], and the *Lawḥ-i-'Álí Páshá*[2] I should be extremely obliged—

Then Edward Browne thanks his friend in Shíráz for repudiating 'any slanders which my enemies might have circulated about me', and identifies the source of these denigrations as two Shaykhís of Kirmán. Shaykhís were remnants of the adherents of Shaykh Aḥmad-i-Aḥsá'í and Siyyid Káẓim-i-Rashtí, forerunners of the Báb, who spoke and wrote of the near approach of the advent of the Qá'im. They owed allegiance to Ḥájí Muḥammad-Karím Khán of Kirmán, a pupil of Siyyid Káẓim, who refused to recognize the Báb and wrote extensively to refute Him. Shaykhís were bitter opponents of the Bábís and later of the Bahá'ís. Browne relates his encounters with them in *A Year Amongst the Persians*. And he has more to say about the two Shaykhís in Kirmán in the letter from which we have been quoting:

they disliked me for obvious reasons, and would have been glad to be able to injure me—One of them was extremely rude and impertinent, and being one day present when a letter was brought to me from your uncle, Hájí Mírzá Muhammad Taḳi[3] [sic], he actually had the impertinence to try and take it from my hand and read it.

Browne recounts this very incident in his book:

I was greatly displeased at the conduct of the aforesaid tutor, Mullá Ghulám Ḥuseyn, on this occasion; for soon after his arrival

[1] Tablet of Bahá'u'lláh addressed to Shaykh Muḥammad-Báqir, a prominent divine of Iṣfahán, who was responsible for the persecution and martyrdom of Bahá'ís. This Tablet is known as *Lawḥ-i-Burhán* (Tablet of Proof). The man who received it was stigmatized as Dhi'b (the Wolf).

[2] 'Álí Páshá was the 'Prime Minister' of the Ottoman Empire, who was implicated in the final banishment of Bahá'u'lláh.

[3] Ḥájí Mírzá Muḥammad-Taqí, son of Ḥájí Siyyid Muḥammad (the maternal uncle of the Báb, for whom Bahá'u'lláh revealed the *Kitáb-i-Íqán* [The Book of Certitude]), though related to Browne's correspondent, was not his uncle. Ḥájí Vakílu'd-Dawlih, a title by which Ḥájí Mírzá Muḥammad-Taqí came to be known in later years, played a major part in the opening years of this century in the construction of the first Bahá'í House of Worship (Mashriqu'l-Adhkár) in 'Ishqábád, in the then Russian Turkistán. His munificence and self-sacrifice were exemplary.

there was placed in my hands a letter from one of my Bábí friends at Yezd, which he, with gross impertinence, requested me to show him. This I naturally declined to do, but he, unabashed, picked up the envelope from the ground where it lay, and began to criticise the superscription. . .[1]

Another point of great interest in this letter is the news which Browne has of Mírzá Muḥammad-Báqir, his talented but highly eccentric teacher of Persian of yesteryears. He had heard from a correspondent in Beirut that Mírzá Muḥammad-Báqir was in Ṭihrán and had gained entry into court circles. After quoting at length from the letter of his Beirut correspondent, which indicated that that extraordinary man was engaged in multifarious activities in the Persian capital, Browne concluded: 'This will shew you how it fares with Mírzá Bāḳir [sic], and that he is still unchanged. I am, however, not without fears that he may once again get into trouble, as he is almost sure to offend someone soon—'

This long letter thus ends:

I hope you will be able some time to obtain for me some further particulars about Hazrat-i-Nuḳta-i-Bayán[2]—the probable date of his birth—his early life, and appearance. I think there must be people at Shíráz who remember him. I am *very very* anxious to learn all that I can about this great and noble man, and I fear that if it is not learned now, it will be lost. I have tried to make out when he was born, and I think, from certain passages in the Beyán [sic], he must have been about 24 years old when he was imprisoned at Mákú, i.e. that he was born about the year A.D. 1824.[3] Hoping soon to hear from you, I remain, with kindest remembrances, ever your sincere friend,[4]

Edward G. Browne.

It is obvious that Edward Browne's primary object was to gather as much information as he could about the Báb. His object was ad-

[1] Browne, *A Year Amongst the Persians*, p. 581.

[2] Ḥaḍrat-i-Nuqṭiy-i-Bayán—His Holiness the Point of Bayán, *i.e.* the Báb.

[3] The Báb was born on Muḥarram 1st 1235 A.H., October 20th 1819 A.D.

[4] This letter is transcribed as Browne wrote it, except that 'and' is spelled out: Browne used a symbol. See Plate I.

mirable. In another letter which we shall examine later, he makes his purpose unequivocally clear. But Edward Browne did not appreciate at the time the significance and the true import of the fulfilment of the short Dispensation of the Báb in the Dispensation of Bahá'u'lláh.

Chapter II

Contact with Ṣubḥ-i-Azal and His Followers

Thus in his search for fresh material Edward Browne entered into correspondence with Mírzá Yaḥyá, Ṣubḥ-i-Azal, who resided in Cyprus and at this point of time was already freed from restriction, because that island had passed out of Turkish rule in 1878 and had become for all practical purposes part of British domains. Free as he was to go into the world and promulgate the Faith of the Báb, Mírzá Yaḥyá chose to remain stationary in Cyprus and receive a pension from the British Government. How different was the action of 'Abdu'l-Bahá three decades later, Who, once freed from the bonds of Ottoman tyranny, undertook a strenuous tour of the Western world to spread the Teachings of Bahá'u'lláh, although He was weighed down with age and physical infirmity.

The first letter from Mírzá Yaḥyá to Edward Browne reached him in August 1889.

But more crucial in forming his subsequent views was Browne's correspondence with Shaykh Aḥmad-i-Rúḥí, which began on Browne's own evidence with a letter dated October 7th 1890, spanned more than three years, and stopped on January 3rd 1894. Prior to Shaykh Aḥmad's violent death in 1896, Browne refers to him in his books as Sheykh A—, a 'learned Ezeli' (sic) resident in Constantinople. It was Shaykh Aḥmad who initiated this correspondence, as Edward Browne has recorded:

> On October 13th, 1890, I received from Constantinople a long letter in Persian, occupying two sheets of writing-paper, and dated Ṣafar 22nd, A.H. 1308 (Oct. 7th, 1890), which letter proved to be from the aforesaid Sheykh A—, with whom I had had no previous communication, and of whose very existence I had till that day been unaware. After apologizing for writing to me without previous introduction or acquaintance, the writer explained

how he had heard of me from Persia and Cyprus, and how he had learned that I had interested myself especially in the Bábí religion. In consequence of this, he said, he had written to me to warn me against certain pretenders to spiritual truth (by whom he meant the Behá'ís [sic]) who had brought discord and dissensions into the bosom of the new faith. After discoursing in this strain at great length, in fine but rather ambiguous language, he continued as follows:[1]

'Now to enable you to understand, not only the words of the Point of Truth (*i.e.* the Báb), or the words of Him called 'The Living' (*i.e.* Ṣubḥ-i-Ezel), but the signs and words of this dispensation in general, there is in my possession a book in the sweet Persian tongue, in very simple style, consisting of about twenty folios or 160 leaves (pp. 320), which sets forth in very easy language the mysteries of this law and its ordinances, and explains the terminology and ideas of these people, in such wise that it will place in your hand a key wherewith to open this treasure-house of the Knowledge of the Names.' The writer then goes on to say that as there is only one copy of this book, and as it has to be jealously kept from the eyes of all save a few, he cannot give the MS., but that if I should like to have it he will either lend it to me for two or three months, that I may make a copy for myself, or will get it copied for me at five francs the folio.

I immediately answered this letter, saying that I should prefer to have a copy made for me in Constantinople, and asking for the name of the book and further particulars about it. In answer to this letter I received on November 10th, 1890, a second communication from Sheykh A—, in which he wrote:[2]

'As to the book of philosophy, its name is *Hasht Bihisht*,[3] and it is written according to the current Persian idiom, so that it may be possible for all to profit by it. Until one has read this book he knows not what the philosophers wished to say, what was and is the object of all these sacred books [which have been revealed] since the beginning which hath no beginning, or what was the design and purpose of the Celestial Tongue in all its past utterances.' The writer added that there was only one other copy of the

[1] Persian text, quoted by Browne, is here omitted.
[2] Persian text, quoted by Browne, omitted. [3] *Eight Paradises*. (H.M.B.)

book besides his own, and that it was in Persia, and was accessible to no one but the owner. . .[1]

A copy was ordered for Edward Browne. When he received fifteen folios, he was told that the rest had been purloined by enemies. He was next informed that *Hasht Bihisht* consisted of two volumes, and that it was the second volume which had been transcribed for him. Eventually, the first volume, too, was copied and sent to Edward Browne. He wished to know the name of the author of *Hasht Bihisht*. To his query Shaykh Aḥmad replied that in the ambit of the Bayán particulars and personalities were of little consequence, yet the information would not be withheld. The contents of *Hasht Bihisht*, he said,

> represent the teachings and sayings of the illustrious Hájí Seyyid Jawád of Kerbelá[2] [sic], who was of the 'First Letters of the Living,' the earliest believers. . . That illustrious personage, now departed, was a pilgrim after truth in these degrees from the time of the late Sheykh Aḥmad of Aḥsá until seven years ago. And he is one whose words are adduced as proof in the *Dalá'il-i-Sab'a*[3] by His Holiness the Point of Revelation [*i.e.* the Báb], who, in the first Epistle which he addressed to him, wrote, 'Peace be upon you, O scion of the prophetic household!' But, inasmuch as during his latter days the strength of that illustrious personage was much impaired and his hands trembled, he was unable to write, wherefore he dictated these words, and one of his disciples wrote them down, but in an illegible hand and on scattered leaves. In these days, having some leisure time in Constantinople, I and this person exerted ourselves to set in order these disordered leaves. In short the original spirit of the contents is his [*i.e.* Seyyid Jawád's], though perhaps the form of words may be ours. Should you desire to mention the name of the author of these two books it is Hájí Seyyid Jawád.[4]

Edward Browne's comment is: 'It is unnecessary to point out the importance of such a work from such a source.'[5] He had every reason

[1] Browne, 'Catalogue and Description of 27 Bábí Manuscripts', *Journal of the Royal Asiatic Society*, vol. XXIV, n.s., pp. 680–2.

[2] Karbilá.

[3] *Seven Proofs*, one of the well-known Works of the Báb. (H.M.B.)

[4] Browne, *J.R.A.S.*, n.s., vol. XXIV, p. 684. [5] *ibid.*, p. 685.

to assess very highly the value of a work ascribed to so eminent a disciple of the Báb. But as we shall see later, Ḥájí Siyyid Javád-i-Karbilá'í was not connected with the authorship of *Hasht Bihisht*. When Browne was writing for the *Journal of the Royal Asiatic Society* in 1892, he had not yet received the whole of the two volumes. The opinion which Edward Browne had already formed of Shaykh Aḥmad's abilities can be measured by this reference to him contained in a letter to Denison Ross, dated '27 September 1891':

> My first introduction to the East was at Constantinople... There are some very learned Persians living there in exile or of choice or for business. If you want I could give you a letter to some of these. One with whom I constantly correspond is in my opinion one of the finest scholars I have come across, and has supplied me with masses of precious information, so that I am inclined to concur in the estimate he gave of himself (quoting from Mutanabbi)
>
> *The night, and the horse-troop, and the desert know me,*
> *And blows and war and the paper and the pen.*[1]

Shaykh Aḥmad-i-Rúḥí was by all accounts a remarkable man: erudite, highly intelligent, possessed of a facile pen. He was, however, an avowed adversary of Bahá'u'lláh, and with no compunction used every means within reach to besmirch His Name. Shaykh Aḥmad and his father, Mullá Muḥammad-Ja'far, the Shaykhu'l-'ulamá, a well-known Muslim divine living in Kirmán, were zealous partisans of Ṣubḥ-i-Azal. There was another citizen of Kirmán, Mírzá 'Abdu'l-Ḥusayn Khán, known as Mírzá Áqá Khán (son of Áqá 'Abdu'r-Raḥím, a wealthy landowner of Bardsír),[2] who was

[1] Ross, *Both Ends of the Candle*, p. 59. John Alexander Chapman who edited Sir Denison Ross's autobiography adds this footnote: 'E.G.B. himself, in his *Literary History of Persia*, vol. I, p. 370, describing the death of this famous Arab poet, has: "Being worsted in the combat, al-Mutanabbi was preparing to take to flight when his slave cried to him: 'Let it never be said that you fled from the combat, you who are the author of this verse:

I am known to the horse-troop, the night and the desert's expanse,
Not more to the paper and pen than the sword and the lance!' " '

[2] Bardsír is a country district in the neighbourhood of Kirmán. Mírzá Áqá Khán's grandfather was an influential supporter of Abu'l-Ḥasan Khán, Aga Khan I, the Imám of the Ismá'ílí sect, who staged a *coup* in 1840. Subsequently, the Aga Khan took refuge in India.

Shay<u>kh</u> Aḥmad's boon companion, and like him eventually married a daughter of Mírzá Yaḥyá. Mírzá Áqá <u>Kh</u>án was also highly accomplished, a talented writer of excellent verse and prose. He went to 'Akká in the lifetime of Bahá'u'lláh, pretending to be a well-wisher and even an adherent, whereas, as attested by Bahá'u'lláh, he was intent on mischief. This was soon proved. He gave out that he had gone to 'Akká to investigate truth, but had returned totally disillusioned. In a famous poem Mírzá Áqá <u>Kh</u>án poses as an ardent Muslim. Elsewhere he even holds the Bábís up to ridicule.

Mírzá Áqá <u>Kh</u>án and Shay<u>kh</u> Aḥmad-i-Rúḥí (incidentally the chief translator[1] of James Morier's *The Adventures of Hajji Baba of Ispahan* into a lucid Persian) left Kirmán together around the year 1885. They visited Iṣfahán, Ṭihrán and Ra<u>sh</u>t. In the capital they

[1] That Shay<u>kh</u> Aḥmad-i-Rúḥí was the translator of *Hajji Baba of Ispahan* had never been in doubt. Colonel D. C. Phillott, who had the Persian version published in Calcutta, in 1905, stated it as a fact. Edward Browne reiterated it in volume IV of his *Literary History of Persia*. Mírzá Muḥammad <u>Kh</u>án-i-Qazvíní, the well-famed critic and bibliographer (d. 1949), affirmed it in his short biographical notice of Shay<u>kh</u> Aḥmad. However Mr H. Kamshad challenges this view in his *Modern Persian Prose Literature* (*op. cit.*), and bases his argument on the contents of a letter from Shay<u>kh</u> Aḥmad to Edward Browne. This letter written in 1892, which also gave Browne the news of the ascension of Bahá'u'lláh in vilest terms, ascribed the translation to Mírzá Ḥabíb-i-Iṣfahání, another learned and versatile Persian *émigré*, resident in Constantinople. Mr Kamshad referring to the publication of the fourth and last volume of *A Literary History of Persia* (1924) writes: 'Perhaps Browne, now old and in poor health, had forgotten Shay<u>kh</u> Aḥmad's plea on behalf of his friend's translation, in a letter received by Browne thirty-two years earlier'. This statement is rather startling. Mr Kamshad formulates an alternative explanation for this lapse on the part of Edward Browne. Because Phillott had committed himself irrevocably in edition after edition, did Browne 'with his customary tact and generosity decide not to correct the colonel's mistake about the real translator?' (p. 23)

Shay<u>kh</u> Aḥmad had his own reasons not to divulge his part in translating James Morier's classic. Mírzá Ḥabíb had, in all certainty, much greater knowledge of English and French than Shay<u>kh</u> Aḥmad whose knowledge of European languages could have been but sketchy. Therefore Shay<u>kh</u> Aḥmad had to rely on Mírzá Ḥabíb's collaboration when he undertook to render into Persian Morier's *Hajji Baba* and Le Sage's *Gil Blas*. Shay<u>kh</u> Maḥmúd, the Afḍalu'l-Mulk, a younger brother of Shay<u>kh</u> Aḥmad, has put it on record that Mírzá Áqá <u>Kh</u>án was also concerned with these translations. Edward Browne's reaction, not responding to Shay<u>kh</u> Aḥmad's suggestions to put in hand the publication of *Hajji Baba* in Persian, might seem strange, but essentially it was not a book which he admired. It should also be noted that Mírzá Ḥabíb outlived Shay<u>kh</u> Aḥmad. The manuscript of the Persian version of *The Adventures of Hajji Baba* was in the possession of Shay<u>kh</u> Aḥmad, and Colonel Phillott received it from his heirs when he held the post of the British Consul in Kirmán.

established valuable relations with grandees. Three years later they arrived at Constantinople, and after a stay of three months proceeded to Cyprus to meet Ṣubḥ-i-Azal. Marriage to his daughters followed soon. Back in Constantinople differences arose between husbands and wives, and Mírzá Yaḥyá's two daughters returned to Cyprus. Sẖayḵẖ Aḥmad and Mírzá Áqá Ḵẖán also left Constantinople; the former went to Baḡẖdád, the latter to Damascus. Later, Sẖayḵẖ Aḥmad moved to Aleppo where he became a close associate of the Persian Consul, and where, strangely enough, he arranged a splendid reception for Ḥájí Muḥammad Ḵẖán, the son of Ḥájí Muḥammad-Karím Ḵẖán-i-Kirmání, who was going on pilgrimage to Mecca. Ḥájí Muḥammad Ḵẖán had inherited from his father both the leadership of the Sẖayḵẖí school, and a deep-seated, bitter hatred of the Báb. It was during this period that Mírzá Áqá Ḵẖán visited 'Akká. Eventually Sẖayḵẖ Aḥmad and Mírzá Áqá Ḵẖán returned to Constantinople and their wives joined them. By the year 1889 they were established in the capital of the Ottoman Empire, engaged in teaching and literary work. Mírzá Áqá Ḵẖán became a sub-editor on the Persian newspaper, *Akẖtar*. That weekly newspaper, which had existed since 1875, reflected liberal views which were anathema to Náṣiri'd-Dín Sẖáh.

Náṣiri'd-Dín Sẖáh who was a tyrant, cruel and avaricious, but not 'ugly' and 'boorish', as described in a recent publication,[1] visited Europe for the third time in 1889. In Munich he met a highly gifted man whose name has gone down in history as the 'Protagonist of Pan-Islamism'. This man was Siyyid Jamálu'd-Dín, generally known as Afḡẖání (native of Afḡẖánistán).[2] This was not their first encounter. Siyyid Jamálu'd-Dín, in his time a stormy petrel of Eastern politics, had lived away from his native land since the days of his boyhood. He had lived in Afḡẖánistán, occupying for a while the post of the first minister; also in Egypt, in Constantinople, in India. He had been expelled from Egypt in 1879 at the instigation of the British representative. When 'Arábí Pásẖá rose in revolt in the

---

[1] S. Jackson, *The Sassoons* (London, 1968).

[2] In fact he was a Persian. His birthplace was Asadábád, near Hamadán in western Persia. This has been hotly and sometimes indignantly contested. The father of the present writer has recorded in his diary that he himself heard Siyyid Jamálu'd-Dín say that he was from Hamadán.

year 1882, Siyyid Jamálu'd-Dín was detained in India, until Egypt had been subdued and pacified. Once allowed to travel, he left Calcutta. After a sojourn of a few months in the United States, he proceeded to London. However, it was a very short visit, and for the next three years he made his home in Paris where, in conjunction with Shaykh Muḥammad 'Abduh, the celebrated Grand Muftí of Egypt, he published a weekly Arabic periodical entitled *al-'Urwathu'l-Wuthqá* (The Indissoluble Link). This paper was bitterly critical of British policies. It was banned in India, and possibly other efforts were made to block its path. However, in 1885, Siyyid Jamálu'd-Dín was once again in London, the guest of Wilfrid Scawen Blunt.[1] Lord Randolph Churchill and Sir Henry Drummond Wolff[2] consulted him, possibly also Lord Salisbury. Siyyid Jamálu'd-Dín, it has been presumed, put certain proposals to British statesmen, directed against Russia, but his terms proved unacceptable. The summer of 1886 saw Siyyid Jamálu'd-Dín in Bushire. He was apparently on his way to Arabia to visit Ibn Rashíd.[3] It is not clear why he changed his mind and proceeded to the port on Persian soil. Was he given an intimation that he would be well received in Persia? What is certain is that at Bushire, where he stayed some three months, an invitation reached him from I'timádu's-Salṭanih, the Minister of Publications, to visit Ṭihrán. This invitation had been formally offered at the express command of Náṣiri'd-Dín Sháh.

But Náṣiri'd-Dín Sháh was soon alarmed, and it was suggested to Siyyid Jamálu'd-Dín that he needed a 'change of air'. He went to St Petersburg (now Leningrad). Before long he had established intimate relations with the Tsarist government. When Náṣiri'd-Dín Sháh embarked on his third European tour, Siyyid Jamálu'd-Dín

[1] Blunt (1840–1922) was an English firebrand, poet, visionary, rebel, 'Arabist', traveller in the East, champion of Eastern nations. He stood by 'Arábí Páshá through thick and thin; went to prison in Ireland for involvement in Irish unrest. Blunt was married to the granddaughter of Lord Byron, and Lady Anne was even more accomplished as an Arabist. A fine portrait of him is drawn in *Wilfrid Scawen Blunt, A Memoir by his Grandson*, the Earl of Lytton (4th Earl), (London, 1961).

[2] British Minister in Persia, 1887–90.

[3] Traditional enemy of Ibn Sa'úd. The late King 'Abdu'l-'Azíz, the founder of Sa'údí Arabia, vanquished the House of Ibn Rashíd, in the early part of this century.

was still at St Petersburg and resolutely refused to meet the S͟háh. He left Russia, determined to avoid Náṣiri'd-Dín S͟háh, but at Munich the two met.

Again here is an imponderable. Why did Siyyid Jamálu'd-Dín agree to try his luck once more in Persia? It is said that the office of the Ṣadr-i-A'ẓam (prime minister) was offered to him; and this at a time when that highly insecure post was occupied by a most ambitious and very able statesman—Mírzá 'Alí-Aṣg͟har K͟hán, the Amínu's-Sulṭán. For whatever reasons, Siyyid Jamálu'd-Dín went to Persia, and soon storms raged round him. He took 'bast' (sanctuary) in the shrine of S͟háh 'Abdu'l-'Aẓím, whence he was dragged out, in defiance of established conventions, and expelled from Írán.

Now began his vendetta against Náṣiri'd-Dín S͟háh. Edward Browne met him in London, in the autumn of 1891. Browne writes,

... I met him by invitation of the late Prince Malkom Khán[1] at the house in Holland Park which, until that eminent diplomatist's quarrel with the Sháh in 1889, was the Persian Legation... During his stay in London he addressed several meetings and wrote sundry articles on 'the Reign of Terror in Persia,' attacking the Sháh's character, and even his sanity, with great violence.[2]

In 1892, Siyyid Jamálu'd-Dín, still vituperating against Náṣiri'd-Dín S͟háh, was received with open arms in Constantinople, by Sulṭán 'Abdu'l-Ḥamíd.[3] The despotic 'Abdu'l-Ḥamíd, although intensely averse to all liberal thought, not only tolerated the presence of a firebrand like Siyyid Jamálu'd-Dín in his capital city, but invited him to reside in Istanbul, and gave him a generous allowance and a house with all its perquisites. The reason was that the Pan-Islamic movement under the direction of Siyyid Jamálu'd-Dín aimed at obtaining recognition of the Ottoman ruler by all Muslims, Sunní and S͟hí'ah alike, as the Head of their Faith.

[1] Prince Malkom K͟hán, the Náẓimu'd-Dawlih, a highly cultured courtier of Armenian extraction, is considered to have been the man who introduced Freemasonry to Írán. This view has been contested. Malkom has been a controversial figure, but his contribution to the Constitutional Movement, and the deep influence of *Qánún*, his newspaper published in London, as well as his other writings is undeniable.

[2] E. G. Browne, *The Persian Revolution* (Cambridge, 1910), p. 11.

[3] 'Abdu'l Ḥamíd II (1842–1918), who came to the throne in 1876 and was deposed in 1909, was called 'Abdul the Damned' in Britain.

Now, Shaykh Aḥmad-i-Rúḥí and Mírzá Áqá Khán attached themselves to the person of Siyyid Jamálu'd-Dín, hostile though he was to the Faith of the Báb. It served their purposes to support and aid and abet Siyyid Jamálu'd-Dín against the reigning monarch of Írán, because the partisans of Ṣubḥ-i-Azal were dedicated to the violent overthrow of the existent order in that land. Bahá'u'lláh, on the other hand, had laid an injunction upon His followers to eschew political action, and shun every manner of violence and rebellion. But Mírzá Yaḥyá and his adherents considered any act not only legitimate, but highly praiseworthy, if it led to the destruction of the detested Qájárs,[1] and the effacement of their foul deeds.

Siyyid Jamálu'd-Dín and his associates wrote to the Shí'ah divines in the holy cities of Karbilá and Najaf, soliciting their active cooperation. Shaykh Aḥmad had a seal made on which these words, in verse form, were inscribed:

> I am the missioner of the unity of Islám,
> Aḥmad-i-Rúḥí is my name.

The following verses from an epic poem[2] by Mírzá Áqá Khán well illustrate his attitude and his part in the campaign levied from Istanbul:

> I desired all good for the Muslims, I adorned my heart with virtue.
> I desired that the Muslims might with one accord gird up their loins in unity,
> Might increase friendship with one another, might expel ancient animosity from their hearts,
> So that honour might increase to them, and that enmity and dissension might be set aside,
> And that, under the auspices of Ḥamíd,[3] a political union might be effected in Islám,
> So that Turk should be Persian, and Persian like Turk, and that duality might no longer remain in these great rulers,
> And that in like manner the learned doctors of 'Iráq should agree in [recognizing] the [Sulṭán as] sovereign supreme,

[1] The ruling dynasty of Persia.
[2] *Námiy-i-Bástán* (The Book of Ancient Times), a history in verse.
[3] [Sulṭán 'Abdu'l-]Ḥamíd.

And should swiftly cleanse their hearts of this animosity, and should no longer talk of who was Sunní and who Shí'í,

. . .

To several well-chosen and virtuous men we wrote many well-renowned letters;
We sent them off to 'Iráq, so that dissension might depart from the realm of Religion.

. . .

From Persia and from 'Iráq they wrote, 'We have washed from our hearts the dust of dissension:
'We will all sacrifice our lives for the Holy Law, we will all swear allegiance to the King of Islám:
'We will forsake the law of estrangement, and will adopt the practice of wisdom:
'Henceforth we will lay low unbelief, and will obtain possession of the world from end to end.'[1]

But the hopes expressed by Mírzá Áqá Khán did not materialize. The Shí'ah world did not recognize Sulṭán 'Abdu'l-Ḥamíd as its overlord. The adversaries of Siyyid Jamálu'd-Dín, who always sought a chance to discredit him—and there were many of them within the ranks of 'Abdu'l-Ḥamíd's entourage—struck and succeeded in inducing the Sulṭán to take away his favours from his guest. Siyyid Jamálu'd-Dín was placed under restrictions. Gradually he was deserted. He died in March 1897, of cancer in the jaw,[2] only ten months after the assassination of Náṣiri'd-Dín Sháh at the hands of Mírzá Muḥammad-Riḍáy-i-Kirmání, one of his disciples.

Siyyid Jamálu'd-Dín's pan-Islamism failed. His political aims remained unfulfilled, although he succeeded in destroying Náṣiri'd-Dín Sháh. His intense hostility to and denigration of the Cause of Bahá'u'lláh, evidenced by the account of the Faith which he wrote for Buṭrus al-Bustání's *Arabic Encyclopaedia*[3] proved of little consequence in the course of time. Bahá'u'lláh mentions him in the *Tablet of the World*, and refers to his articles in Bustání's Encyclopaedia and in Egyptian papers as 'astonishing'. Siyyid Jamálu'd-Dín,

[1] Translation by E. G. Browne in *The Persian Revolution*, pp. 412–13.
[2] It has been said that he was poisoned.
[3] The *Dá'iratu'l-Ma'árif*, published in Beirut.

He states, sent copies of his Paris periodical to 'Akká so as to show a measure of friendliness, 'to atone for the past'; and He comments, 'We kept silent regarding him'.

When the Sulṭán's favours waned and Siyyid Jamálu'd-Dín was discarded as an instrument of 'Abdu'l-Ḥamíd's aggrandizement, the Sublime Porte[1] responded to the urgent representations of the Persian Ambassador, 'Aláu'l-Mulk, and agreed to put Shaykh Aḥmad and Mírzá Áqá Khán under arrest. Maḥmúd Páshá, the Chief of the police in Istanbul, was promised in return the extradition of the Armenians who had fled to Persia. Ḥájí Mírzá Ḥasan Khán, the Khabíru'l-Mulk, at one time Persian Consul-general in Istanbul, another disciple of Siyyid Jamálu'd-Dín, was detained as well, and the Siyyid could not save them. They were moved to Trebizond and kept in prison there until Náṣiri'd-Dín Sháh, tyrannical and obscurantist to the end, perished by an assassin's bullet on May 1st 1896. Then they were dispatched to Tabríz, the seat of the Crown Prince of Persia, where the cowardly incumbent of that office, Muḥammad-'Alí Mírzá, had them beheaded on July 15th, while he watched. Thus died Shaykh Aḥmad-i-Rúḥí, who was in a large measure responsible for the course that Edward Granville Browne was to pursue.

Náṣiri'd-Dín Sháh was about to celebrate the completion of his half-a-century[2] of disastrous reign. On the eve of his jubilee he drove to the shrine of Sháh 'Abdu'l-'Aẓím, in the vicinity of his capital. Within the inner sanctum Mírẓá Muḥammad-Riḍá, driven to desperation by cruelties he had suffered, and heartened by the counsel of Siyyid Jamálu'd-Dín, awaited him. There can be no doubt that the assassination of Náṣiri'd-Dín Sháh was engineered by Siyyid Jamálu'd-Dín. Edward Browne reports him to have said, when they met in London: '. . . no reform was to be hoped for until six or seven heads had been cut off; "the first . . . must be Náṣiru'd-Dín Sháh's, and the second the Amínu's-Sulṭán's."'[3] The assassin is reported to have stated during his interrogation:

[1] The seat of the Ottoman Government. [2] In lunar reckoning.
[3] Browne, *The Persian Revolution*, p. 45.

You know how, when Sayyid Jamálu'd-Dín came to this city, all the people, of every class and kind, alike in Ṭihrán and in Sháh 'Abdu'l-'Aẓím, came to see him and wait upon him, and how they listened to his discourses. And since all that he said was said for God and for the public good, everyone profited and was charmed by his words. Thus did he sow the seed of these high ideas in the fallow ground of men's hearts, and the people awoke and came to their senses. Now everyone holds the same views that I do; but I swear by God Most High and Almighty, who is the Creator of Sayyid Jamálu'd-Dín and of all mankind, that no one, save myself and the Sayyid, was aware of this idea of mine or of my intention to kill the Sháh.[1]

Náṣiri'd-Dín Sháh lay dead in a shrine outside his capital, murdered. His chief minister (Ṣadr-i-A'ẓam), the Amínu's-Sulṭán, saw immediately the enormity of the situation. The internal security of the state was gravely menaced. The Sháh had merely fainted, he told the royal entourage, and with the help of a few close to him, carried the corpse to the carriage, sat beside it, and drove at full speed back to Ṭihrán. Once precautions had been taken, and the Crown Prince, Muẓaffari'd-Dín Mírzá, resident in Tabríz, had been informed, the news of the assassination rapidly spread. And suspicion fell upon the Bahá'ís. In Cairo where the great Bahá'í teacher, fearless and erudite Mírzá Abu'l-Faḍl of Gulpáygán lived, ugly noises were made by some members of the Persian community, urged on by an adversary of long standing—Dr Mírzá Muḥammad-Mihdí Khán, the Za'ímu'd-Dawlih,[2] whose father had seen the Báb in Tabríz. However, the Persian Consul-general in Cairo was a wise man, a moderate, courageous official. He counselled his countrymen to be patient and await definite, reliable news. Sinister developments were averted, and the accusers of the Bahá'ís were confounded.

But in Ṭihrán itself innocent blood was shed. On the morrow of

[1] *ibid.*, p. 73.

[2] He owned and edited a Persian journal in Cairo, entitled *Ḥikmat*. Ra'ísu'l-Ḥukamá (the Chief of the Physicians or Philosophers) was another title which he enjoyed. In 1903 the Arabic Cairo Press of al Manár published a book by him on the Faith of the Báb and Bahá'u'lláh. It was meant to be a refutation and carried the title: *Miftáḥu Bábi'l-Abwáb* (The Key to the Gate of Gates), thus appearing to be a work of history. It is almost unknown now.

the Sh͟áh's death, Ḥájibu'd-Dawlih, a brutal courtier who had convinced himself of the guilt of the Bahá'ís, rushed into the gaol where a number of them languished. Among them was Mírzá 'Alí-Muḥammad whom Bahá'u'lláh had named Varqá (Dove)—able poet, eloquent, constant, serene; also his twelve-year-old son, Rúḥu'lláh. Ḥájibu'd-Dawlih tore open Varqá's abdomen with a dagger, and then turned to the young boy to torment him with his jibes and to offer him a way of escape. Rúḥu'lláh spurned the offer. They half-strangled him, revived him, taunted him to recant. But recant he would not. All that he desired was to join his father, to die for the Faith of Bahá'u'lláh.

It is interesting to note the reaction of the British Press to the news of the assassination of Náṣiri'd-Dín Sh͟áh. On May 2nd, *The Times* stated that a Bábí had murdered the Sh͟áh and concluded that the Bábí Movement was 'a sort of religious crusade against the corruption of public and private manners'. Within the next four days the *Scotsman*, the *Manchester Guardian*, the *Graphic*, the *Spectator*, the *Morning Post*, the *Pioneer*, unanimously made the same allegation. To cap it all, an illustrated paper, called *St Paul's*, produced on May 16th the picture of a dervish looking crazed and unkempt, with the caption: 'A Babi, one of the sect to which the Shah's assassin belongs'.

Letters from Edward Browne appeared in *The Times* on May 6th, and in the *Daily News* on May 12th, refuting what the press had alleged.

Apart from the writings of Edward Browne, there was the monumental work of Lord Curzon, *Persia and the Persian Question*,[1] with its admirable account of the Faith of the Báb and Bahá'u'lláh, which the press could have consulted, to learn what this Faith was and what it stood for.[2]

[1] George N. Curzon, *Persia and the Persian Question* (Longmans, Green and Co., London, 1892).

[2] It is astonishing how uninformed or misinformed have men in the centre of affairs been about the Bábí and the Bahá'í Faiths. In 1917, the War Cabinet decided that Edwin Montagu, Secretary of State for India, member of a very distinguished Jewish family, should visit India, consult individuals and parties con-

Bahá'u'lláh states in His *Tablet of Ṭarázát* that,

> Newspapers are as a mirror which is endowed with hearing, sight and speech; they are a wonderful phenomenon and a great matter. But it behoveth the writers thereof to be sanctified from the prejudice of egotism and desire and to be adorned with the ornament of equity and justice; they must inquire into matters as much as possible, in order that they may be informed of the real facts, and commit the same to writing.[1]

Western writers were still in the closing decade of the century applying the term 'Babi' to the followers of Bahá'u'lláh, and continued to do so for many years, an error for which Edward Browne bears no little responsibility. But when some of them went to the length of calling Siyyid Jamálu'd-Dín, who was evidently hostile to the new Faith, 'a Babi leader', they were following the ways of the

---

cerned, and work out in conjunction with Lord Chelmsford, the Viceroy, the next step in Indian political evolution. The Montagu-Chelmsford Reforms that resulted initiated a system of dyarchy. Whilst in India, Edwin Montagu kept a special diary for the sake of informing the Prime Minister, David Lloyd George, of the day-to-day progress of his mission. After Montagu's premature death it was edited by his wife, Lady Venetia (née Stanley), and was published in 1930, by William Heinemann under the title, *An Indian Diary*. On page 64, from Delhi, Tuesday, November 27th 1917, we read: '. . . I had an interview with Dobbs, who is going to administer Baluchistan. . . I have asked the Viceroy to send home to Curzon his letter about Persia. It is truly sad that, owing to our desire to placate Russia—what a bad bargain we made!—we have alienated the Persian democrats. Dobbs told me that nearly 70 per cent. of the Persians openly or in secret belong to their new religion. In about the year 1857 a young man appeared, who was crucified, shot at, and finally killed by the Persians. One of his disciples then said that he was God, and that the man who had been killed was a forerunner something like John the Baptist. He preaches a sort of internationalism, and they are all deserting Mohammedanism, and these are the democrats whom we are losing. He gave me instances to show that their belief in this creed was so great that it even conquered their rapacity, which is one of their chief characteristics.'

Next on page 99, from Calcutta, Monday, December 10th 1917: '. . . Then I had a few words with the Persian Consul-general, who denies the story of the growth of the new religion in Persia that Dobbs told me about in Delhi. He himself said cynically: "there is no room for new religions; if I lose my old one, I never want another".'

The Persian Consul-general mentioned above was Miftáḥu's-Salṭanih.

Sir Henry R. C. Dobbs, K.C.M.G., K.C.I.E., of Indian Political Department, succeeded Sir Percy Z. Cox, G.C.M.G., K.C.S.I., as the High Commissioner in the mandated territory of 'Iráq, in 1923.

[1] See *The Bahá'í Revelation* (London, 1955), p. 151.

ignorant in Persia who dubbed anyone unorthodox with the term 'Bábí'. Even a scholar as meticulous as Colonel D. C. Phillott, who wrote very knowledgeably on Persian grammar, fell into this error. No wonder then that a leading article in the *Morning Post* of May 11th 1896 referred to Siyyid Jamálu'd-Dín as 'the Afghan who is the recognized leader of the Babi'.

NOTE

Since this book was first published, further evidence has been brought to the author's attention regarding the identity of the translator into Persian of *The Adventures of Hajji Baba of Ispahan*, which necessitates some correction of p. 22 and footnote.

In his introduction to a recent edition of this work (Ṭihrán, 1348/1969), Siyyid Muḥammad-'Alí Jamálzádih has given a clear outline of the available facts. Although it is true that Colonel D. C. Phillott in the first edition of this work attributes the Persian translation to Shaykh Aḥmad-i-Rúḥí, it appears that his only ground for doing so was that he had received the manuscript from among Shaykh Aḥmad's papers that were sent to Kirmán after the latter's execution in Tabríz. Jamálzádih states that on his first sight of the book, he suspected from the style of the translation that it was the work of Mírzá Ḥabíb-i-Iṣfahání, but was at a loss to explain this since Mírzá Ḥabíb had known French and had translated works from French into Persian, but had not known English. Then there came to light the letter from Shaykh Aḥmad to Prof. Brown which Dr Kamshad quotes (see p. 22 footnote). That this letter is not in fact from Shaykh Aḥmad-i-Rúhí but from his colleague Mírzá Áqá Khán-i-Kirmání, is proved not only by the handwriting evidence, which Jamálzádih cites, but because, further on in the letter, its author states that he went to 'Akká. Such a statement could only have come from Mírzá Áqá Khán. Another piece of the jigsaw fell into place when Jamálzádih discovered that a French translation of *Hajji Baba* had been published in the same year, 1824, as the original English edition. This then must have been the text that Mírzá Ḥabíb used (and indeed Mírzá Áqá Khán's letter states that Mírzá Ḥabíb translated the book from the French, a statement which was thought to have been a slip of the pen). The final and conclusive evidence was the discovery in 1961 by the late Mojtaba Minovi in the University Library of Istanbul of a manuscript of this translation in Mírzá Ḥabíb's handwriting, confirming that he himself was the translator.

Also, since the first edition of this book was published, much interesting information has come to light regarding the activities and intrigues of Mírzá Áqá Khán and Shaykh Aḥmad-i-Rúhí in Istanbul, part of this from the letters of Mírzá Áqá Khán to Malkam Khán that are in the Bibliothèque Nationale, Paris. A full account will be found in the chapter, 'The Azalís in Constantinople', in the present author's work, *Bahá'u'lláh, The King of Glory* (George Ronald, 1980).

February 1980

Chapter III

Succession to the Báb and the Position of Ṣubḥ-i-Azal

Hashṯ Bihishṯ or *Eight Paradises* is essentially an apologia for Mírzá Yaḥyá. Although Mírzá Áqá Khán has been named its author, the hand of Shaykh Aḥmad-i-Rúḥí is more apparent in its composition. On occasions it is scurrilous. Edward Browne gave an adequate résumé of the main argument of *Hashṯ Bihishṯ*, and the charges it levels against Bahá'u'lláh, in the appendices to his translation of *A Traveller's Narrative*. It is past belief that a man as intelligent as Shaykh Aḥmad could have used such flimsy arguments and made such threadbare statements that can be easily exposed. For example, men are named as Letters of the Living[1] who could not possibly have belonged to that group, men such as Mullá Rajab-'Alíy-i-Qahír and Siyyid 'Alíy-i-'Arab. These are listed as supporters of Ṣubḥ-i-Azal, alleged to have been assassinated by the Bahá'ís. Browne himself points out a number of misstatements, or rather false statements, and says of murders attributed by the author of *Hashṯ Bihishṯ*, and by Ṣubḥ-i-Azal, to the followers of Bahá'u'lláh:

> It seemed to me a kind of ingratitude even to repeat such charges against those from whom I myself have experienced nothing but kindness, and in most of whom the outward signs of virtue and disinterested benevolence were apparent in a high degree. Yet no feeling of personal gratitude or friendship can justify the historian (whose sole desire should be to sift and assort all statements with a view to eliciting the truth) in the suppression of any important document which may throw light on the object of his study. Such an action would be worse than ingratitude; it would be treason to Truth. These charges are either true or false. If they be true

[1] The first eighteen believers in the Báb who constituted His original disciples, first of whom was Mullá Ḥusayn-i-Bushrú'í, the Bábu'l-Báb (Gate to the Gate), and the last, Mullá Muḥammad-'Alíy-i-Bárfurúshí, entitled Quddús.

(which I ardently hope is not the case) our whole view of the tendencies and probable influences of Behá's [sic] teaching must necessarily be greatly modified, for of what use are the noblest and most humane utterances if they be associated with deeds such as are here alleged? If, on the other hand, they be false, further investigation will without doubt conclusively prove their falsity, and make it impossible that their shadow should hereafter darken the page of Bábí history. In either case it is of the utmost importance that they should be confronted, and, to this end, that they should be fully stated. Inasmuch as the *Hasht Bihisht* only fell into my hands as I was beginning to write this note, and as several of the charges alleged in it against the Behá'ís [sic] are new to me, I regret that I cannot at present offer any important evidence either for their support or their refutation.[1]

It is a fact that three Azalís were murdered by a few Bahá'ís in 'Akká. That shameful deed brought great sorrow to Bahá'u'lláh, added to the rigours of His incarceration and evoked poignant lamentation from His pen. He wrote: 'My captivity cannot harm Me. That which can harm Me is the conduct of those who love Me, who claim to be related to Me, and yet perpetrate what causeth My heart and My pen to groan.'[2]

Nothing can justify murder. But let it be said that one of these three Azalís was Siyyid Muḥammad-i-Iṣfahání,[3] the tempter and

[1] Browne (ed.), *A Traveller's Narrative*, vol. II, pp. 364–5.

[2] Cited by Shoghi Effendi in *God Passes By*, p. 190.

[3] The epithet, 'Antichrist of the Bahá'í Revelation', was applied by the Guardian of the Faith to Siyyid Muḥammad-i-Iṣfahání. An incident which should be particularly noted is his marriage to the sister of Mullá Rajab-'Alí, entitled Qahír, one of the Bábís whose murder in 'Iráq the author of *Hasht Bihisht* imputed to the Bahá'ís. Edward Browne seems convinced that Bahá'ís were guilty of that murder. He states it as a fact in his *Materials for the Study of the Bábí Religion* (p. 199), a book which we shall consider later. In the same work he even names the murderer: 'Náṣir the 'Arab, one of the followers of Bahá'u'lláh' (p. 220).

The Báb, during His six-months' sojourn in Iṣfahán, took as His second wife a sister of the said Mullá Rajab-'Alí, named Fáṭimih. Perforce, she had to stay in her native town, when the Báb was taken away from Iṣfahán by the orders of Ḥájí Mírzá Áqásí, the Grand Vizier of Muḥammad Sháh (father of Náṣiri'd-Dín Sháh). The Báb had forbidden marriage, after Him, with either of his two wives. In spite of this interdiction, Mírzá Yaḥyá married the sister of Mullá Rajab-'Alí, but later divorced her, and gave her in marriage to Siyyid Muḥammad. Partisans of Ṣubḥ-i-Azal have denied that he ever married the sister of Mullá Rajab-'Alí.

For years Edward Browne corresponded with an Azalí, resident in Ṭihrán, the evil genius of Mírzá Yaḥyá. Another one was Áqá-Ján Big, ex-artillery officer in the Turkish army, whose plottings in Constantinople led to Bahá'u'lláh's exile in 1868. When the Ottoman Government decided to banish Bahá'u'lláh to 'Akká, and Azal to Cyprus, it also decreed that four Bahá'ís should accompany Azal, and a num-

---

whom he knew as Mírzá Muṣṭafá, referred to in *Materials for the Study of the Bábí Religion* (p. 228) as 'the Bábí scribe to whom I am indebted for so many interesting works and documents'. This man provided Browne with a Tablet of 'Abdu'l-Bahá, addressed to Mírzá 'Alí-Akbar Khán-i-Mílání, the Muḥibu's-Sulṭán (for many years secretary of the central Bahá'í Spiritual Assembly of Ṭihrán), and a refutation of the same Tablet, written by himself. In an accompanying letter he told Browne for the first time that his real name was Ismá'íl, that he was a 'Ṣabbágh' (dyer) by profession, and came originally from Sidih near Iṣfahán. He also disclosed in that letter the fact that his teacher had been Mullá Zaynu'l-'Ábidín, entitled Zaynu'l-Muqarrabín, one of many Bábís who went to Baghdád and turned away with dismay from Mírzá Yaḥyá. Then he met Bahá'u'lláh, to Whom he gave lifelong devotion.

Mírzá Muṣṭafá or Ismá'íl-i-Ṣabbágh-i-Sidihí had previously written a retort to Zaynu'l-Muqarrabín. Mírzá Muṣṭafá's letter, and Edward Browne's note attached to it which contains this sentence: 'Received on September 15, 1922, from Dr. Sa'íd through his son Samuel Sa'íd', indicate that the intermediary for the dispatch of manuscripts to Cambridge was Dr Sa'íd Khán-i-Kurdistání, a well-known and highly respected physician of Ṭihrán. Dr Sa'íd Khán was a convert from Islám to Christianity, active and ardent in the interests of Christian mission. The present writer, having been Dr Sa'íd Khán's patient in his boyhood, remembers him well; the doctor's probity was unquestionable. Mírzá Muṣṭafá had been at pains, in his refutation of 'Abdu'l-Bahá's Tablet, to prove that Mírzá Yaḥyá did not marry the sister of Mullá Rajab-'Alí. To set the seal on this assertion he produced a statement by that lady who was said, in 1914, to be eighty-five years of age. That was in lunar reckoning. Edward Browne mentions that she died in December 1916, eighty-four years old (*Materials, op. cit.*, p. 220, n. 2). The statement attributed to her is fairly long. The gist of it is that subsequent to the martyrdom of the Báb, she and her family suffered persecution; the Imám-i-Jum'ih of Iṣfahán (a high clerical dignitary) was demanding her hand. Her brother took her to 'Iráq where, in the company of Siyyid Muḥammad, they visited Mírzá Yaḥyá who showed her a Testament in the handwriting of the Báb, in which He had called her by a title known to no one else, had commanded her to obey Mírzá Yaḥyá; then Mírzá Yaḥyá had wed her to Siyyid Muḥammad. Furthermore, the alleged statement accuses Bahá'u'lláh of having sought to marry her.

In the margin of p. 66 of Mírzá Muṣṭafá's manuscript, now preserved in the University Library of Cambridge, we read: 'For years this lady was my patient in Ṭihrán. I questioned her regarding many matters that were important and of historical interest, and recorded what she told me. I heard it from herself that she obeyed Azal and became his wife, and remained married to him for a month, then Azal's wives became abusive and very quarrelsome, so "His Holiness was forced to separate me from himself, and gave me to Siyyid Muḥammad". Sa'íd, Kurdistání physician, 20. IV. 22.'

ber of Azalís should be included amongst the companions of Bahá'u'lláh (see p. 82). That was how Azalís came to be in 'Akká. They did not rest for a moment in the pursuit of their designs. They used every means to denigrate Bahá'u'lláh, to place His life in jeopardy, to cast aspersions on His followers, to harm them in every possible manner. Once released from confinement in the citadel, Siyyid Muḥammad and Áqá-Ján Big lodged in a house over the second city-gate to keep a spying-post. Whenever they spotted the arrival of a Bahá'í from the outer world, they would immediately run to the authorities with the information. Many a Bahá'í who had toiled and travelled for months to reach 'Akká, was thus foiled and deprived of the bounty that he eagerly sought. Bahá'u'lláh, on the other hand, constantly counselled His people to desist from retaliation, to put away all thoughts of revenge. He even sent away to Beirut an Arab Bahá'í who was inclined to strike back. But just as two Bábís, demented with grief, attempted the life of Náṣiri'd-Dín-Sh͟áh in 1852, seven Bahá'ís, sorely tried and driven to desperation, chose to disregard the injunction of Bahá'u'lláh, and, in the dead of night, killed Siyyid Muḥammad and Áqá-Ján Big and Mírzá Riḍá-Qulí. Pandemonium broke loose in the wake of this despicable deed, and Bahá'u'lláh suffered grievously.

Mírzá Riḍá-Qulíy-i-Tafrish͟í, the third Azalí murdered in 'Akká, was a brother-in-law of Ṣubḥ-i-Azal. He and his brother, Mírzá Naṣru'lláh, were in the employment of the French Legation in Ṭihrán. Towards the end of the Adrianople period, their sister, Badrí-Ján, deserted her husband, Mírzá Yaḥyá, and took refuge in the house where Bahá'u'lláh resided. No amount of persuasion could induce her to return to her husband's home. It became inevitable to summon her brothers from Ṭihrán to take her to Persia. Mírzá Riḍá-Qulí, Mírzá Naṣru'lláh, his son Mírzá Faḍlu'lláh and their servant Áqá 'Aẓím-i-Tafrish͟í reached Adrianople, about the time when the intrigues in Constantinople were beginning to bear fruit. Mírzá Naṣru'lláh died of a chest complaint in Adrianople. The author of *Hash͟t Bihish͟t*, as usual, makes the bald statement that the Bahá'ís poisoned him, but gives no proof. Why they should have done so remains obscure.

Badrí-Ján sent her two daughters back to their father. Some years later, the elder was married to <u>Sh</u>ay<u>kh</u> Aḥmad-i-Rúḥí, and the younger to Mírzá Áqá <u>Kh</u>án. Badrí-Ján, her remaining brother, her nephew, and Áqá 'Aẓím were included in the band of exiles that accompanied Bahá'u'lláh to 'Akká. 'Aẓím became a devoted adherent of Bahá'u'lláh, and served Him faithfully. Badrí-Ján and her brother repeatedly broke their word to Bahá'u'lláh. Finally Mírzá Riḍá-Qulí threw in his lot with Siyyid Muḥammad and Áqá-Ján Big. That was how he came to be murdered.

Edward Browne had ample knowledge of that horrendous episode in 'Akká when he was preparing *A Traveller's Narrative* for press. But what of other charges of murder? We shall later come back to them. Marshalling of unsifted material makes poor history. Admittedly, it was not easy for Edward Browne, under the prevailing circumstances, to try to test the veracity of the vicious statements made by the author of *Ha<u>sh</u>t Bihi<u>sh</u>t*. However, the outstanding and tragic fact was that Edward Browne had convinced himself that Mírzá Yaḥyá, Ṣubḥ-i-Azal, was the legitimate successor of the Báb, specifically appointed to that office by the martyred Prophet of <u>Sh</u>íráz Himself. This is what he writes on this crucial issue:

> In my opinion it is proved beyond all doubt that the Báb ere his death chose him as his successor. . .[1]

Was there in existence a specific document, written by the Báb, explicitly naming Mírzá Yaḥyá as His successor? No, there was not, and such a document has never existed. Edward Browne, anxious to learn all that he could about Ṣubḥ-i-Azal, wrote to two British officials in Cyprus: Mr C. D. Cobham, Commissioner at Larnaca, and Captain Young, Commissioner at Famagusta. The latter visited Ṣubḥ-i-Azal the day after he had received Edward Browne's letter. In Browne's own words:

> . . . he succeeded so well in winning *Ṣubḥ-i-Ezel's* [sic] confidence that with this first letter (dated July 28th, 1889) he was able to forward a MS. of one of the Báb's works, whereof, so far as I know, no copy had previously reached Europe. Through Captain Young I was also able to address directly to *Ṣubḥ-i-Ezel* letters containing questions on numerous matters connected with the history, doc-

[1] Browne (ed.), *A Traveller's Narrative*, vol. II, p. 350.

trine, and literature of the Bábís, to all of which letters I received most full and courteous replies.[1]

The manuscript mentioned by Browne was a Tablet of the Báb, on which the whole case of Azal's succession rests. Reference to this document first appeared in the October 1889 issue of the *Journal of the Royal Asiatic Society*. Browne wrote:

> ... Captain Young succeeded in obtaining from Ṣubḥ-i-Ezel ... a document of great historical interest, viz. the appointment of Ṣubḥ-i-Ezel by the Báb as his successor. This is, I believe, copied directly from the original in Ṣubḥ-i-Ezel's possession. As it is too valuable to be omitted, ... I subjoin the text and translation.

Then Browne went on to say:

> The document from which the above text is taken is endorsed by Captain Young as follows: '*Copy of Appointment of Ṣubḥ-i-Ezel as Báb's successor, original written by Báb*' ... This document furnishes us with the grounds whereon *Ṣubḥ-i-Ezel's* claims to be the Báb's vicegerent are based.[2]

Next, Edward Browne published a facsimile of the document in the handwriting of Mírzá Yaḥyá, which he had received from Captain Young, in the appendices (IV, no. 2, facing p. 426) to his translation of the *New History of the Báb* (1893) with slight variants in translation.

The translation offered here by the present writer is fundamentally based on Browne's versions:

> God is Most Great with the utmost Greatness. This is a letter from the presence of God, the Sovereign Protector, the Self-Subsistent; to God, the Sovereign Protector, the Self-Subsistent. Say: 'All originate from God.' Say: 'All return unto God.' This is a letter from 'Alí before Nabíl,[3] the Remembrance of God unto

[1] Browne (ed.), *A Traveller's Narrative*, vol. II, xix. In a later work, *New History of the Báb* (Cambridge, 1893), Browne gave the date of his first letter from Captain Young as July 29th (p. 421).

[2] *J.R.A.S.*, n.s., vol. XXI, pp. 996–7.

[3] Nabíl numerically equals 'Muḥammad'. Therefore 'Alí before Nabíl reads as ''Alí-Muḥammad' which is the name of the Báb.

the worlds; unto him whose name is equivalent to the name of the Sole One,[1] the Remembrance of God unto the worlds. Say: 'Verily all originate from the Point of Bayan.[2] O Name of the Sole One, preserve what hath been revealed in the *Bayán*, and what hath been commanded; for verily thou art a Great Way of Truth'.

The original of the Tablet, said to have been written by the Báb, was shown to Edward Browne when, as we shall observe later, he visited Mírzá Yaḥyá in Cyprus.[3] The question is not whether this Tablet is genuine or not.[4] The point is that nowhere in this document is there any mention of successorship.

Furthermore, the Bahá'ís have never questioned the fact that immediately after the execution of the Báb, leadership, even if nominal, was accorded to Mírzá Yaḥyá. He was the 'recognized chief of the Bábí community'.[5] He was one of the Mirrors[6] of the Bábí Dispensation. But over and above any argument and consideration stand two supreme facts: the awesome injunctions of the Báb concerning 'Him Whom God shall make manifest', and the erratic behaviour of Ṣubḥ-i-Azal throughout the years of transition.

The Báb had made it unequivocally clear that the primary purpose of His Mission was to herald the advent of 'Him Whom God shall manifest'. The worth of every man and everything, including His own book, the *Bayán*, a Book which Bahá'u'lláh characterized as the 'Mother Book', He had made dependent upon approval by the Manifestation of God Who was to come after Him. 'The *Bayán* and whosoever is therein,' He had written, 'revolve round the saying of "Him Whom God shall make manifest" . . .'[7] 'A thousand perusals

[1] 'Vaḥíd' (the Sole One) is numerically equal to twenty-eight, and so is Yaḥyá which is the name of Ṣubḥ-i-Azal.

[2] The Báb was 'Nuqṭiy-i-Bayán'—The Point of the Bayán. *Bayán* is His revealed Book.

[3] *J.R.A.S.*, n.s., vol. XXIX, p. 763.

[4] The copy in the handwriting of Ṣubḥ-i-Azal has a word added in the left-hand corner: 'Imḍá'—signature. In a recently published facsimile which is in a handwriting closely resembling the handwriting of the Báb, there is no 'signature', but a seal affixed which reads: 'verily I am the Proof of God and His Light'.

[5] Shoghi Effendi, *God Passes By*, p. 163.

[6] 'Mir'át'—Mirror—was a distinction conferred by the Báb.

[7] Cited by Shoghi Effendi, *The Dispensation of Bahá'u'lláh* (London, 1947), p. 9.

of the *Bayán*,' He had stated, 'cannot equal the perusal of a single verse' to be revealed by 'Him Whom God shall make manifest'.[1] Referring to Himself He had said that He was 'a ring upon the hand of Him Whom God shall make manifest', Who 'turneth it as He pleaseth, for whatsoever He pleaseth, and through whatsoever He pleaseth'.[2] He had given a grave warning to His followers to be vigilant lest they deprive themselves of recognising that 'Remnant of God', that 'Omnipotent Master', that 'Essence of Being', the 'Crimson, all-encompassing Light', the 'Lord of the visible and invisible', that 'sole Object of all previous Revelations, including the Revelation of the Qá'im[3] Himself.'[4] Indeed such was the weight of His admonition that He told Siyyid Yaḥyá of Dáráb, entitled Vaḥíd, one of the most outstanding of His followers, a man of vast erudition and eminence:

> By the righteousness of Him Whose power causeth the seed to germinate and Who breatheth the spirit of life into all things, were I to be assured that in the day of His manifestation thou wilt deny Him, I would unhesitatingly disown thee and repudiate thy faith. . . If, on the other hand, I be told that a Christian, who beareth no allegiance to My Faith, will believe in Him, the same will I regard as the apple of Mine Eye.[5]

'The first servant to believe in Him',[6] the Báb had named Himself. The entirety of His book, the *Bayán*, is one continuous, unbroken paean of praise and adoration, submission to and glorifying of 'Him Whom God shall make manifest'.

How did Mírzá Yaḥyá, Ṣubḥ-i-Azal, 'the nominee of the Báb', act when his Master was put to death, when almost all the Báb's disciples had fallen? He fled the capital. He went about the countryside in disguise. In an account which he wrote during 1889, in answer to Browne's questions, Mírzá Yaḥyá admitted his flight, although Ṭihrán was his abode. He stated that the Báb had said: 'Azal

[1] Cited *The Dispensation of Bahá'u'lláh*, p. 9.
[2] Cited by Shoghi Effendi, *God Passes By*, p. 98.
[3] 'The One Who Arises'—the Promised One of Islám—the Báb.
[4] Quotation and appellations preceding cited *God Passes By*, p. 97.
[5] Cited *The Dispensation of Bahá'u'lláh*, p. 9.
[6] Cited *God Passes By*, p. 98.

should preserve himself'. Browne published that account (happily so) in the appendices to his translation of the *New History of the Báb*. Very fortunate indeed was it that Edward Browne put into print this narration by Mírzá Yaḥyá, both in the original Persian and in an English translation, because it is incontestable evidence of the stature of Ṣubḥ-i-Azal. Strange that Browne should have rated it so highly. In the Introduction to the aforementioned book, he says this about it:

> On the importance of such an account coming from such a source it is unnecessary to dwell: it is almost as though we had a narrative of the first beginnings of Islám told by 'Ali ibn Abí Ṭalib.[1] That so valuable a document deserved publication will, I should think, be questioned by no one.[2]

What does this document, thus eulogized, add to our knowledge of the inception of the Faith of the Báb and its fortunes? It is there in print for any impartial reader to judge. Those whose mother tongue is Persian, and those who are well acquainted with that language, will find it particularly revealing to read Ṣubḥ-i-Azal's composition. He wrote a great deal, and the British Museum has volumes of his writings in manuscript. They are there available for all to examine and evaluate.

[1] 'Alí, the cousin and son-in-law of Muḥammad. (H.M.B.)
[2] Browne (ed.), *New History of the Báb*, lii.

Chapter IV

The Bábí Community in the Period of Transition

After the martyrdom of the Báb, the people who bore His Name were completely demoralized. Not only had the Báb met a cruel death, but those, also, who were outstanding amongst His followers had, with few exceptions, perished. Mullá Ḥusayn, the first to believe in Him; Quddús, the one who had primacy in the company of His first eighteen disciples—the Letters of the Living; the great Vaḥíd who, sent by Muḥammad Sháh to investigate the claims of the Báb, had given Him his unreserved allegiance; Mullá Muḥammad-'Alí of Zanján, entitled Ḥujjat (Proof), who, even prior to his conversion to the new Faith, had confounded the ranks of opponents, and had won signal favours from the Sháh; Ḥájí Mírzá Siyyid 'Alí, the uncle who had acted as a father to the Báb during His tender years of orphanhood; and a host of others equally heroic and dedicated, had fallen prey to blazing hatred. Ṭáhirih, the silver-tongued, undaunted poetess of Qazvín, one of the Letters of the Living (the only one of them who had not seen the Báb in person, and had believed in Him from afar), was held in captivity. Bahá'u'lláh had gone to 'Iráq on pilgrimage to the holy cities there.

The community of the Báb, harassed and hounded and heartbroken, was in grave danger of succumbing to forces of reckless nihilism within its own ranks. A not inconsiderable number of Bábís had taken the attitude that no law, human or divine, was any longer binding on them. Many of them felt that their incandescent faith, their unshakeable loyalty to the memory of their martyred Master, their total dedication to the truth of a new Theophany had freed them from the shackles of the law. Some of the charges brought against them by their opponents had sound basis in fact. Faced with a prospect utterly bleak, their vision was dimmed and their sense of values distorted.

It was only natural, in circumstances of frustrated hope and mounting agony, and in view of the clear, emphatic promise given them by the Báb regarding the near advent of 'Him Whom God shall make manifest', that a number of them should step forth almost in a state of self-hypnosis, to claim to be the One for whose sake the Báb had joyously shed His blood, to proclaim that they had come to rescue a community stunned by adversity from the abyss of despair and degradation. Again it was natural that they should find adherents, that some should gladly rally round them, for it was a guiding hand, a wise counsellor that the Bábís desperately needed. Hardly any of these self-styled 'Manifestations of God' were men of guile or greed or ambition. As tensions increased their number rose to the high figure of twenty-five. One of them was an Indian named Siyyid Baṣír, a man of unbounded courage and zeal, who eventually met the death of a martyr. A wilful prince of the House of Qájár inflicted atrocious tortures upon him to which he succumbed. Another was Mírzá Asadu'lláh of Khuy, whom the Báb had named Dayyán,[1] and acknowledged as the 'Third Letter to believe in Him Whom God shall make manifest'. Even more, the Báb had referred to him as the repository of trust and knowledge of God.

At the time when Bahá'u'lláh had left Baghdád to dwell in the mountains of the north, Dayyán approached Mírzá Yaḥyá and was greatly disappointed. Then it was that he advanced a claim of his own in support of which he wrote a treatise, and sent a copy to Mírzá Yaḥyá. The response of Ṣubḥ-i-Azal was to condemn him to death. He wrote a book which he called *Mustayqiẓ*[2] (Sleeper Awakened) to denounce Dayyán and Siyyid Ibráhím-i-Khalíl, another prominent Bábí, who had also turned away from him. Dayyán was castigated as 'Abu'sh-Shurúr'—the father of iniquities. Browne writes of this accusation:

> Ṣubḥ-i-Azal . . . not only reviles him in the coarsest language, but expresses surprise that his adherents 'sit silent in their places and do not transfix him with their spears,' or 'rend his bowels with their hands.'[3]

[1] Asadu'lláh and Dayyán (Judge, also Rewarder) are numerically equivalent.
[2] There are copies of this book in the British Museum.
[3] E. G. Browne, *Materials for the Study of the Bábí Religion* (Cambridge, 1918), p. 218.

When Bahá'u'lláh returned to Baghdád, Dayyán met Him and renounced his claim. But the sentence of death pronounced by Ṣubḥ-i-Azal was carried out by his servant, Mírzá Muḥammad-i-Mázindarání. Mírzá 'Alí-Akbar, a cousin of the Báb, who was devoted to Dayyán, was also murdered. The author of *Hasht Bihisht* states that the Mázindarání assassin was a servant of Bahá'u'lláh, and Dayyán was eliminated by His orders. Apart from the evidence of *Mustayqiẓ* which fixes the guilt, we have the curious testimony of a tract attributed to a sister of Ṣubḥ-i-Azal. In an effort to make her see how untenable the position of Mírzá Yaḥyá was, 'Abdu'l-Bahá wrote her a long Letter, in which He addressed her as 'O my affectionate Aunt'. The aforementioned tract is her supposed answer to 'Abdu'l-Bahá's Tablet. *Risáliy-i-'Ammih*—The Aunt's Treatise—as it has come to be known, is an apologia for Ṣubḥ-i-Azal. No attempt is made to conceal his responsibility for the death of Dayyán. On the contrary, it is affirmed and justified on the grounds that Dayyán was 'the father of iniquities'.

Another claimant to the station of 'Him Whom God shall make manifest' was Mullá Muḥammad-i-Zarandí, later surnamed Nabíl-i-A'ẓam. But in a short while he saw the gravity of his aberration, went to Bahá'u'lláh to beg forgiveness, and became the prime historian and chronicler of the Ministry of the Báb and of Bahá'u'lláh.

Where was Mírzá Yaḥyá, Ṣubḥ-i-Azal, 'the nominee of the Báb', during all this period of bewildering confusion? What did he do to protect the Faith and the people so hopelessly adrift? Nothing at all. He was either in hiding or going about heavily disguised. There is no shred of evidence of any attempt on his part to rehabilitate the Bábí community. And even if he had exerted himself to any constructive action, his ineptitude was starkly evident, since the Bábís were sinking and sinking fast.

When (as mentioned earlier) in August 1852, two young Bábís, demented with grief, made an abortive attempt on the life of Náṣiri'd-Dín Sháh, and plunged their fellow-believers into a holocaust,[1] it was Bahá'u'lláh Who calmly rode towards the Sovereign's camp and faced the fury of a people shocked by outrage, and it was Ṣubḥ-i-Azal who fled in terror. True, he was young, but much younger was

[1] See *Bahá'u'lláh* by H. M. Balyuzi (London, 1963), pp. 15–19.

'Abdu'l-Bahá when His Father went to the mountains of Kurdistán and heavy responsibilities were laid upon His shoulders. When at last, in the relative security of the Ottoman realms, Ṣubḥ-i-Azal resorted to action, it was to block the healing efforts of his Brother. Goaded and directed by Siyyid Muḥammad-i-Iṣfahání he took a course which could only end in his own ruin.

The appallingly debased and decimated ranks of the followers of the Báb needed a firm hand to gather them together, to show them the purpose of their Faith, to recreate their lives. How misinformed and misconstrued is this comment of Edward Browne on the demeanour and behaviour of Ṣubḥ-i-Azal:

> Such firmness Ṣubḥ-i-Ezel [sic], a peace-loving, contemplative, gentle soul, wholly devoted to the memory of his beloved Master, caring little for authority, and incapable of self-assertion, seems to have altogether lacked. Even while at Baghdad he lived a life of almost complete seclusion, leaving the direction of affairs in the hands of his half-brother Behá'u'lláh[1] [sic], a man of much more resolute and ambitious character, who thus gradually became the most prominent figure and the moving spirit of the sect. For a considerable time Behá'u'lláh continued to do all that he did in the name, and ostensibly by the instructions, of Ṣubḥ-i-Ezel; but after a while, though at what precise date is still uncertain, the idea seems to have entered his mind that he might as well become actually, as he already was virtually, the Pontiff of the Church whose destinies he controlled.[2]

This statement does not bear close examination. If the Báb had laid a mandate upon Ṣubḥ-i-Azal, and had explicitly appointed him to be His successor, then what was it that was required of him? Was it to leave the Bábí community to its own devices at a time when it was plagued with lawlessness, obsessed with wildest notions, torn with factious strife? Even the book designed to extol Ṣubḥ-i-Azal, the *Nuqṭatu'l-Káf* to which Edward Browne attached great significance, and which we shall have to examine later in some detail, bears witness to the confused condition of the Bábí community. The Head of a Faith has to care for it.

[1] See *Traveller's Narrative*, vol. ii, pp. 356–8. (E.G.B.)
[2] Browne (ed.), *New History of the Báb*, xxi.

Edward Browne has certainly overlooked certain facts in that statement. It was known that the Bahá'ís celebrated a festival in April, called by them the greatest of all festivals, which marked Bahá'u'lláh's departure from Baghdád in 1863 and the Declaration of His Mission. It was also known that Bahá'u'lláh revealed the *Kitáb-i-Íqán* (The Book of Certitude) in Baghdád in 1862.[1] Was that matchless Book given to the world at the bidding of Mírzá Yaḥyá and in his name? Were *The Seven Valleys* and *The Hidden Words* composed in Baghdád at the instance and according to the directions of Ṣubḥ-i-Azal? Whose fame was it that was spreading far and wide? Who was it that the Government of Írán was so anxious, so insistent to have removed from the vicinity of its territories to a remote part of the Ottoman Empire? Against Whom were the denunciations of the Shí'ah divines of 'Iráq and Írán so vociferously directed? Whose destruction were they encompassing? For Whose removal from Baghdád were they exerting ever-increasing pressure on the Government of Náṣiri'd-Dín Sháh? It was Bahá'u'lláh, not Ṣubḥ-i-Azal.

A document[2] obtained by Monsieur A.-L.-M. Nicolas, First Dragoman of the French Legation in Ṭihrán, a diligent translator of the Works of the Báb, the author of a book on His Life and Mission[3] and a man faithfully devoted to His imperishable memory—a document which was published in later years by Edward Browne himself[4]—makes it indisputably clear Who was maligned and Whose banishment was demanded by the Persian Foreign Minister. This document is a letter, dated May 10th 1862, written by Mírzá Sa'íd Khán, the Mu'ṭaminu'l-Mulk, the Foreign Minister of Persia, to Ḥájí Mírzá Ḥusayn Khán, the Mushíru'd-Dawlih, the Ambassador of Persia in Istanbul. The Person named was Bahá'u'lláh. Ṣubḥ-i-Azal was nowhere in the picture. In his letter to Browne, Nicolas particularly pointed out this fact.

[1] In the second volume of *A Literary History of Persia From Firdawsí to Sa'dí* (London, 1906), Edward Browne made this reference to the *Kitáb-i-Íqán*: 'Yet simplicity and directness is to be found in modern as well as in ancient writers of Persian verse and prose; the Íqán ("Assurance") of the Bábís, written by Bahá'u'lláh about A.D. 1859, is as concise and strong in style as the *Chahár Maqála*, composed some seven centuries earlier. . .' (p. 89)

[2] A copy of this document was sent to Edward Browne in March 1902.

[3] A.-L.-M. Nicolas, *Seyyèd Ali Mohammed dit le Bâb*, 2 vols. (Paris, 1905).

[4] Browne, *Materials for the Study of the Bábí Religion*, pp. 279–83.

After referring to attempts made to extirpate the Bábís, Mírzá Sa'íd Khán says:

> But by chance, and through the ill-considered policy of former officials, one of them, to wit Mírzá Ḥusayn 'Alí of Núr,[1] obtained release from the *Anbár* prison and permission to reside in the neighbourhood of the Shrines . . . whither he departed. From that time until now, as your Excellency is aware, he is in Baghdád, and at no time hath he ceased from secretly corrupting and misleading foolish persons and ignorant weaklings.[2]

It was Bahá'u'lláh Who was exiled from Baghdád to Constantinople, from Constantinople to Adrianople.

And the cardinal point is this: Bahá'u'lláh never put forward any claim under any guise that He was the successor to the Báb. What He proclaimed to the Bábís, and later to the world at large, was the supreme fact that He was the One Whose advent the Báb had heralded—He Whom God shall make manifest, so designated by the Báb—the Redeemer of Latter Days promised to man in all his Scriptures. Therefore Edward Browne's observation that some time or other 'the idea seems to have entered his mind that he might as well become actually, as he already was virtually, the Pontiff of the Church whose destinies he controlled' is well wide of the mark. Bahá'u'lláh was not taking on the tasks and responsibilities of the 'Pontiff' of a 'Church'. He was simply stating that He was a Manifestation of God—His Vicegerent on this earth.

This further remark by Browne in the same Introduction to the *New History of the Báb* is yet another proof that he was losing sight of the true nature of the events he was investigating:

> Now once admitting Behá's [sic] right to assume this position of supremacy at all, there can be no question that these changes were beneficial and salutary. The original doctrine of the Báb, fascinating as it was to Persians of a certain disposition, was utterly unfitted for the bulk of mankind, and could never by any possibility have taken any root outside Persia.[3]

[1] *i.e.*, Bahá'u'lláh.

[2] Translated by E. G. Browne, *Materials for the Study of the Bábí Religion*, pp. 283–4.

[3] Browne (ed.), *New History of the Báb*, xxv–xxvi.

The crux of this argument is this, that Bahá'u'lláh set about altering and adapting the teachings of the Báb so as to make them more palatable to the rest of the world, which cannot be maintained, because Bahá'u'lláh was not a reformer within the Bábí Dispensation, but an independent Manifestation of God.

Browne writes of Bahá'u'lláh as 'one who is the object of a devotion and love which kings might envy and emperors sigh for in vain!'[1] When he visited 'Akká, he saw that Bahá'u'lláh was surrounded by devoted followers. He testifies that apart from his family, Ṣubḥ-i-Azal was almost alone in Famagusta. He admits that in Adrianople Ṣubḥ-i-Azal was left with hardly anyone to support him. In Persia there were a number who looked upon him as the successor to the Báb. But, as we shall see later, when this man to whom they owed allegiance died, not a single one of them was in Cyprus to give him a burial in accordance with the prescription of the Bábí Faith. He died deserted.

However, the defection of Mírzá Yaḥyá, Ṣubḥ-i-Azal, in the words of the Guardian of the Bahá'í Faith, 'perplexed and confused the friends and supporters of Bahá'u'lláh, and seriously damaged the prestige of the Faith in the eyes of its western admirers'.[2] One of these was Edward Granville Browne.

[1] Browne (ed.), *A Traveller's Narrative*, vol. II, xl.
[2] Shoghi Effendi, *God Passes By*, p. 163.

Chapter V

Edward Browne's Visit to Cyprus and 'Akká

In his papers that appeared in the *Journal of the Royal Asiatic Society* for the year 1889,[1] Edward Browne seemed to express the view that if Bahá'u'lláh were indeed 'He Whom God shall make manifest' He was entitled to supersede Ṣubḥ-i-Azal. In the course of the following years his approach to the problem underwent a noticeable change, amply evidenced by his Introduction to the *New History of the Báb*. During those years he had been corresponding with Mírzá Yaḥyá and with Shaykh Aḥmad-i-Rúḥí. We should now go back to Browne's own story.

Reference was made previously (p. 17) to a letter from Edward Browne to the father of the present writer. It was written from Newcastle-on-Tyne, dated January 1st 1889. After making extensive and very pertinent inquiries about the life of the Báb and the early days of the Bábí Faith, Browne writes:[2]

> I am very anxious to get as accurate an account of all the details connected with the Bábí movement as possible, for in my eyes the whole seems one of the most interesting and important events that has occurred since the rise of Christianity and Muhammadanism —and I feel it my duty, as well as pleasure, to try [sic] as far as in me lies, to try [sic] and bring the matter to the notice of my countrymen: that they may consider it—With a view to this, I have promised to give an account of it at Cambridge next term, and also later in the year here—I am very sorry I could not go to '*Akká* this time, but I mean to go there on the first opportunity; perhaps in the summer, though that is a bad time, I fancy. Do you think I

[1] Published under the title, 'The Bábís of Persia', *J.R.A.S.*, n.s., vol. XXI, pp. 485–526 and pp. 881–1009.

[2] This letter transcribed as Browne wrote it, except to spell 'and': Browne usually used a symbol.

should be allowed to see BEHÁ[1] if I went there? At any rate I might see 'Abbás Efendí[2]—At any rate I feel it incumbent on me to go there, for I cannot rest till I have sifted the matter to the bottom . . . I wish very much that while in Persia I could have seen anyone who had seen the Báb or conversed with him . . . if you could help me to collect any more detailed information about these matters, I should be very grateful to you, and I am sure you would be doing a most valuable work, and one which will get more and more difficult every year—For suppose anyone could tell us more about the childhood and early life and appearance of Christ, for instance, how glad we should be to know it. Now it is impossible to find out much, but in the case of the Báb it *is* possible, and I feel that *now that it is possible* it may be neglected, and some day, when Bábíism has perhaps become the national religion of Persia, and many men long to know more of its Founder, it will be impossible —So let us earn the thanks of posterity, and provide against that day now—[3]

As mentioned earlier, Edward Browne met Ḥájí Mírzá Ḥaydar-'Alí for an hour or two in Iṣfahán. He now, in this letter, inquires about him, and what he writes is another testimony to the scale of the endeavours of that redoubtable Bahá'í teacher and the charm of his person:

. . . have you seen *Hájí Mírzá Hyder* [sic] *'Alí* whom I met at Isfahán? I heard the last time I was at Teherán that he had gone to Shíráz—If you see him, please remember me to him most kindly, and say how very much I regretted not seeing him again, for I heard at Yezd[4] on my return that he was then at Teherán, and that I should see him there, and on my arrival there I heard to my great disappointment that he had just left for *Iṣfahán* and *Shíráz*, and that indeed he had been in *Ḳum*[5] when I was—

The father of the present writer helped Browne to go to 'Akká and attain the presence of Bahá'u'lláh. But prior to visiting 'Akká Browne went to Cyprus to meet Ṣubḥ-i-Azal. He landed at Larnaca on March 19th 1890. Thence he proceeded to Famagusta where Ṣubḥ-i-Azal resided. British authorities there had made necessary

[1] Bahá'u'lláh. [2] 'Abdu'l-Bahá. [3] See Plates II–IV. [4] Yazd. [5] Qum.

arrangements for Browne. In the company of Captain Young, Commissioner at Famagusta, he called on Mírzá Yaḥyá.

> . . . we ascended to an upper room, [he writes] where a venerable and benevolent-looking old man of about sixty years of age, somewhat below the middle height, with ample forehead on which the traces of care and anxiety were apparent, clear searching blue eyes, and long grey beard, rose and advanced to meet us. Before that mild and dignified countenance I involuntarily bowed myself with unfeigned respect; for at length my long-cherished desire was fulfilled, and I stood face to face with Mírzá Yaḥyá *Ṣubḥ-i-Ezel* [sic] ('the Morning of Eternity'), the appointed successor of the Báb, the fourth 'Letter' of the 'First Unity.'[1]

By referring to Ṣubḥ-i-Azal as the fourth '"Letter" of the "First Unity"' Browne obviously meant that he was one of the 'Letters of the Living'. But Mírzá Yaḥyá did not belong and could not have belonged to that first group of the disciples of the Báb, all of whom are known by name, and all of whom with the sole exception of Ṭáhirih (Qurratu'l-'Ayn), travelled to Shíráz in their quest, met the Báb in Person and acknowledged Him as the 'Lord of the Age'. Mírzá Yaḥyá never met the Báb. Indeed the Báb laid an injunction on Mullá Ḥusayn, the first to believe in Him, not to divulge to anyone that he had reached the end of his quest, and that others must come unbidden and unprompted to seek and find Him.

Elsewhere Browne states that the Báb Himself was the First in the hierarchy of the Bábí Church. Next to Him stood Quddús (the eighteenth of the 'Letters of the Living', who had primacy in that company), the third being Mullá Ḥusayn, and the fourth Mírzá Yaḥyá. The Báb suffering martyrdom, and Quddús and Mullá Ḥusayn having already met the same fate, Mírzá Yaḥyá moved to the top and 'became the recognized chief of the sect'.[2] It is a fantastic construction which bears no relation to actual fact.

> During the fortnight which I spent at Famagusta [says Browne] I visited *Ṣubḥ-i-Ezel* daily, remaining with him as a rule from two or three o'clock in the afternoon until sunset. Lack of space forbids me from describing in detail and consecutive order the con-

[1] Browne (ed.), *A Traveller's Narrative*, vol. II, xxiv. [2] *ibid.*, p. 95, n. 1.

versations which took place on these occasions. Note-book and pencil in hand I sat before him day by day; and every evening I returned to Varoshia[1] with a rich store of new facts, most of which will be found recorded in the notes wherewith I have striven to illustrate or check the statements advanced in the following pages.[2]

On April 5th Edward Browne embarked for Beirut. The father of the present writer had apprised a cousin in Beirut of Browne's desire to visit 'Akká. This relative, an Afnán (that is, a member of the family of the Báb), was married to a daughter of Bahá'u'lláh. Browne refers to him in his Introduction to *A Traveller's Narrative* as 'the Bábí agent at Beyrout'. In the same Introduction he relates how he reached 'Akká, and how he was taken to the Mansion of Bahjí, some way out of 'Akká, where Bahá'u'lláh resided.

There is in the possession of the present writer a Tablet addressed to his father, wherein Bahá'u'lláh mentions Edward Browne, though not by name. To the best of this writer's knowledge, this is the only Tablet of Bahá'u'lláh in which there is a reference to Edward Browne.[3] Here is the relevant passage:

> Your letter was sent to the Supreme Threshold by Afnán on whom be My glory. The youth mentioned therein attained Our presence. Although this Wronged One had not consorted for many years past with people from foreign lands, We received him on several occasions. Portents of sincerity could be discerned on his visage. We beseech God to aid him in such undertakings which would be conducive to the effacement of mischief and the promotion of the betterment of the world. He is the Hearing, the Prayer-Answering. Afnán will write and give you details.

Also in the possession of the present writer is the letter which Ḥájí Siyyid 'Alí Afnán[4] wrote on this occasion. His account differs from Browne's on a point or two. Browne mentions that he travelled from Beirut to 'Akká overland, in the company of Eyres, the British Vice-consul, whereas Ḥájí Siyyid 'Alí states that he came by sea. Oversight by Afnán in writing 'Baḥr' (sea) instead of 'Barr' (land)

[1] Suburb of Famagusta. [2] Browne, *A Traveller's Narrative*, vol. II, xxiv–xxv.
[3] Reproduced as frontispiece. [4] 'The Bábí agent at Beyrout'.

could easily account for this. However, these are minor details. Afnán records that when Browne reached 'Akká, Bahá'u'lláh was in Haifa, and that He returned to Bahjí the following day. This explains why Browne was given hospitality for one night in 'Akká, in the home of a Bahá'í, before being conducted to the Mansion of Bahjí.[1]

> So here at *Behjé* [sic] was I installed as a guest [he writes], in the very midst of all that Bábíism accounts most noble and most holy; and here did I spend five most memorable days, during which I enjoyed unparalleled and unhoped-for opportunities of holding intercourse with those who are the very fountain-heads of that mighty and wondrous spirit which works with invisible but ever-increasing force for the transformation and quickening of a people who slumber in a sleep like unto death. It was in truth a strange and moving experience, but one whereof I despair of conveying any save the feeblest impression. I might, indeed, strive to describe in greater detail the faces and forms which surrounded me, the conversation to which I was privileged to listen, the solemn melodious reading of the sacred books, the general sense of harmony and content which pervaded the place, and the fragrant shady gardens whither in the afternoon we sometimes repaired; but all this was as nought in comparison with the spiritual atmosphere with which I was encompassed . . . The spirit which pervades the Bábís is such that it can hardly fail to affect most powerfully all subjected to its influence. It may appal or attract: it cannot be ignored or disregarded. Let those who have not seen disbelieve me if they will; but, should that spirit once reveal itself to them, they will experience an emotion which they are not likely to forget.[2]

Siyyid 'Alí Afnán corroborates in his letter Browne's statement that books were presented to him. Browne names two books: a

[1] 'It was in that same mansion that the distinguished Orientalist, Prof. E. G. Browne of Cambridge, was granted his four successive interviews with Bahá'u'lláh, during the five days he was His guest at Bahjí (April 15–20, 1890), interviews immortalized by the Exile's historic declaration that "*these fruitless strifes, these ruinous wars shall pass away and the 'Most Great Peace' shall come.*"' (Shoghi Effendi, the Guardian of the Bahá'í Faith, in *God Passes By*, p. 194.)

[2] Browne (ed.), *A Traveller's Narrative*, vol. II, xxxviii–xxxix.

manuscript copy of the *Kitáb-i-Íqán* (The Book of Certitude) in the handwriting of Zaynu'l-Muqarrabín, and a copy of *A Traveller's Narrative*, also in manuscript form, in the handwriting of the same eminent scribe. Afnán mentions a copy of the Tablet to Náṣiri'd-Dín S͟háh as being among the gifts. He corroborates, too, the statement of Browne that they travelled back together overland to Beirut, which they reached on April 22nd.

On May 1st, Edward Browne was 'back in Cambridge'. 'So ended,' he writes, 'a most interesting, most successful, and most pleasant journey.'[1]

Edward Browne visited Cyprus, and Ṣubḥ-i-Azal, once again in 1896 (March 18th–25th). It was during this second visit that Ṣubḥ-i-Azal produced for Browne's inspection the original document which, he maintained, had conferred apostolic succession upon him.[2]

There had been a long pause in the correspondence between Edward Browne and Ṣubḥ-i-Azal, a hiatus of four years.[3] The reason has not been explained. Subsequent to that second visit Browne received one more letter from Mírzá Yaḥyá, dated May 17th of the same year. Then their correspondence totally ceased.[4]

[1] Browne (ed.), *A Traveller's Narrative*, vol. II, xliii.
[2] *J.R.A.S.*, vol. XXIX, 1897, pp. 761–3. [3] *ibid.*, p. 762.
[4] Browne, *Materials for the Study of the Bábí Religion*, p. 234.

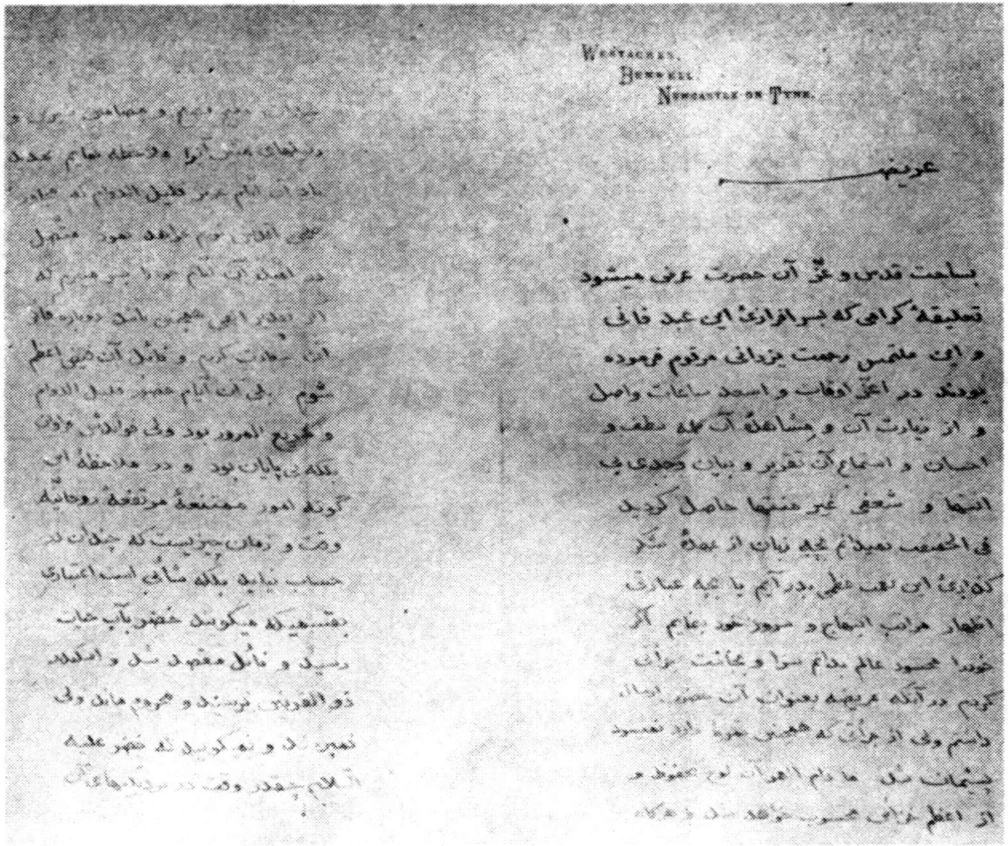
Westacres,
Benwell,
Newcastle on Tyne.

عزیزم

V. LETTER TO ‘ABDU’L-BAHÁ
From Edward Browne
Dated September 11th 1890

VI. SECOND HALF OF LETTER TO 'ABDU'L-BAHÁ From Edward Browne

Chapter VI

'A Traveller's Narrative'

On his return to Cambridge, Edward Granville Browne set out to translate *A Traveller's Narrative*. The English version, bearing the title: *A Traveller's Narrative written to illustrate The Episode of the Báb*, and a facsimile reproduction of the original manuscript (which was presented to Browne in Bahjí), were published by the Cambridge University Press in two volumes in 1891. At the time Browne did not know that this history of the Faith of the Báb and Bahá'u'lláh was from the pen of 'Abdu'l-Bahá, although he learned this fact at a later date.[1] In the Introduction to his translation Browne related the story of how he came to be interested in the Mission of the Báb, and gave a comprehensive account of his visit to Cyprus and 'Akká. To the text he appended copious notes.

On the eve of publication Browne wrote to 'Abdu'l-Bahá:

As I wrote previously the translation of the history bestowed upon me is completed. A third of it is printed, and it is hoped that within two or three months the completed work will be in the hands of the public. Every effort has been made to better and improve the translation. Even subsequent to the correction of the translation in manuscript, the printed version was two or three times compared with the original manuscript, so that, God willing, it shall be befitting, and acceptable for both correctness and eloquence. Of these two one is not acceptable without the other. It is certain that the production of this authentic and comprehensive history, which supersedes all that previous historians have written about this Cause, will greatly benefit all the people, and will lead to further seeking and enquiry. If my journey had no other result than this it would still be the most profitable of journeys.[2]

These are the opening words of the Introduction:

[1] Browne (ed.), *New History of the Bab*, xxxi.

[2] Extract from letter dated September 11th 1890. See Plates v–vi.

This book is the history of a proscribed and persecuted sect written by one of themselves. After suffering in silence for nigh upon half a century, they at length find voice to tell their tale and offer their apology. Of this voice I am the interpreter.[1]

The pen-portrait of Bahá'u'lláh which is included in the Introduction is indeed unique and must be quoted in full:

> During the morning of the day after my installation at *Behjé*[2] one of Behá's[3] younger sons entered the room where I was sitting and beckoned to me to follow him. I did so, and was conducted through passages and rooms at which I scarcely had time to glance to a spacious hall, paved, so far as I remember (for my mind was occupied with other thoughts) with a mosaic of marble. Before a curtain suspended from the wall of this great ante-chamber my conductor paused for a moment while I removed my shoes. Then, with a quick movement of the hand, he withdrew, and, as I passed, replaced the curtain; and I found myself in a large apartment, along the upper end of which ran a low divan, while on the side opposite to the door were placed two or three chairs. Though I dimly suspected whither I was going and whom I was to behold (for no distinct intimation had been given to me), a second or two elapsed ere, with a throb of wonder and awe, I became definitely conscious that the room was not untenanted. In the corner where the divan met the wall sat a wondrous and venerable figure, crowned with a felt head-dress of the kind called *táj*[4] by dervishes (but of unusual height and make), round the base of which was wound a small white turban. The face of him on whom I gazed I can never forget, though I cannot describe it. Those piercing eyes seemed to read one's very soul; power and authority sat on that ample brow; while the deep lines on the forehead and face implied an age which the jet-black hair and beard flowing down in indistinguishable luxuriance almost to the waist seemed to belie. No need to ask in whose presence I stood, as I bowed myself before one who is the object of a devotion and love which kings might envy and emperors sigh for in vain!
>
> A mild dignified voice bade me be seated, and then continued:

[1] Browne (ed.), *A Traveller's Narrative*, vol. II, vii. [2] Bahjí.
[3] Bahá'u'lláh. [4] Crown. (H.M.B.)

—'Praise be to God that thou hast attained! . . . Thou hast come to see a prisoner and an exile. . . We desire but the good of the world and the happiness of the nations; yet they deem us a stirrer up of strife and sedition worthy of bondage and banishment. . . That all nations should become one in faith and all men as brothers; that the bonds of affection and unity between the sons of men should be strengthened; that diversity of religion should cease, and differences of race be annulled—what harm is there in this? . . . Yet so it shall be; these fruitless strifes, these ruinous wars shall pass away, and the "Most Great Peace" shall come. . . Do not you in Europe need this also? Is not this that which Christ foretold? . . . Yet do we see your kings and rulers lavishing their treasures more freely on means for the destruction of the human race than on that which would conduce to the happiness of mankind. . . These strifes and this bloodshed and discord must cease, and all men be as one kindred and one family. . . Let not a man glory in this, that he loves his country; let him rather glory in this, that he loves his kind. . .'

Such, so far as I can recall them, were the words which, besides many others, I heard from Behá. Let those who read them consider well with themselves whether such doctrines merit death and bonds, and whether the world is more likely to gain or lose by their diffusion.[1]

Equally vivid and arresting was the impression left on his mind when the young orientalist met 'Abdu'l-Bahá:

Seldom have I seen one whose appearance impressed me more. A tall strongly-built man holding himself straight as an arrow, with white turban and raiment, long black locks reaching almost to the shoulder, broad powerful forehead indicating a strong intellect combined with an unswerving will, eyes keen as a hawk's, and strongly-marked but pleasing features—such was my first impression of 'Abbás Efendi, 'the master' (*Aḳá*)[2] as he *par excellence* is called by the Bábís. Subsequent conversation with him served only to heighten the respect with which his appearance had from the first inspired me. One more eloquent of speech, more ready of argument, more apt of illustration, more intimately acquainted

[1] Browne (ed.), *A Traveller's Narrative*, vol. II, xxxix–xl. [2] Áqá.

with the sacred books of the Jews, the Christians, and the Muhammadans, could, I should think, scarcely be found even amongst the eloquent, ready, and subtle race to which he belongs. These qualities, combined with a bearing at once majestic and genial, made me cease to wonder at the influence and esteem which he enjoyed even beyond the circle of his father's followers. About the greatness of this man and his power no one who had seen him could entertain a doubt.[1]

This further comment in the same Introduction, with its note of certainty, must be particularly underlined:

Of one thing there can, in my opinion, be but little doubt: the future (if Bábíism, as I most firmly believe, has a future) belongs to Behá[2] and his successors and followers.[3]

Edward Browne's enthusiasm and eagerness earned him a drubbing from a pompous reviewer in *The Oxford Magazine*. It could not but have damped his spirits. That he was deeply wounded by the superior manner, the ill-informed and injudicious remarks of that reviewer is apparent in what he wrote, more than a decade later, in his long Introduction to *Abbas Effendi, His Life and Teachings*, by Myron H. Phelps of the New York Bar. That reference to his rough treatment ought to be quoted in full, because of the light that it throws on his reticence in later years. Furthermore, it illustrates the type of shoddy reviewing which is not uncommon, even when undertaken by the eminent, and provides evidence of a genre of ignorance, which unhappily persists. Browne wrote:

To the study of the Bábí religion I was irresistibly attracted, even before I undertook my journey to Persia in 1887–88, by the vivid and masterly narrative of its birth and baptism of blood contained in the Comte de Gobineau's *Religions et Philosophies dans l'Asie Centrale*—a narrative which no one interested in the Bábí (or, if the term be preferred, Behá'í) faith, or indeed in the history of religion in general, should on any account omit to read with careful attention. My enthusiasm was still further increased by what

[1] Browne (ed.), *A Traveller's Narrative*, vol. II, xxxvi.
[2] Bahá'u'lláh. (H.M.B.)
[3] Browne (ed.), *A Traveller's Narrative*, vol. II, xviii.

I saw of the Bábís in Persia, and by my subsequent visits to Behá'u'lláh at 'Akká and to his rival, Subh-i-Ezel, at Famagusta in Cyprus. It was under the influence of this enthusiasm that I penned the Introduction (several times cited by Mr. Phelps in the following pages) to my translation of the *Traveller's Narrative*, a book which had been much more eagerly and widely read in America than in this country, where, at the time of its publication, the very name of the Bábís, now grown familiar even to readers of the daily press, was hardly known to the general public. This enthusiasm, condoned, if not shared, by many kindly critics and reviewers, exposed me to a somewhat savage attack in the *Oxford Magazine*, an attack concluding with the assertion that my Introduction displayed 'a personal attitude almost inconceivable in a rational European, and a style unpardonable in a University teacher'.

Increasing age and experience, (more's the pity!) are apt enough, even without the assistance of the *Oxford Magazine*, to modify our enthusiasms; but in this case at least time has so far vindicated my judgment against that of my Oxford reviewer that he could scarcely now maintain, as he formerly asserted, that the Bábí religion 'had affected the least important part of the Moslem world, and that not deeply'. Every one who is in the slightest degree conversant with the actual state of things in Persia now recognises that the number and influence of the Bábís in that country is immensely greater than it was fifteen years ago. . .

The following comes in a footnote:

The review in question appeared in the *Oxford Magazine* of May 25, 1892, p. 394. Amongst many other egregious observations, the reviewer, 'speaking candidly as a layman,' considers that 'the history of a recent sect which has affected the least important part of the Moslem world (nor that part very deeply) and is founded on a personal claim which will not bear investigation for a moment' is 'quite unworthy of the learning and labour which' (he was kind enough to say) 'the author has brought to bear upon it'; while, in the closing sentence, he 'records his belief that the prominence given to the "Báb" in this book is an absurd violation of historical perspective; and the translation of the *Traveller's*

Narrative a waste of the powers and opportunities of a Persian scholar'.

I am well aware that it is generally considered undignified and improper for an author to take any notice of his critics, or even to admit that their strictures have caused him more than a momentary vexation; and towards the more irresponsible reviewers of journals which do not profess to represent the opinions of a cultivated circle such indifference is undoubtedly the correct attitude. But the *Oxford Magazine*—at any rate outside Oxford—is supposed to be a serious exponent of the ideas and judgments of that University; and one has the right to expect that a work treating of an Oriental religious movement shall not be judged by one who, however great an authority he may be on classical archaeology, knows so little even of Islám that he can speak of the originator of the Wahhábí movement as 'Wahháb' (and even this he incorrectly writes, 'Waháb'); a blunder comparable to that of the Turkish journalist who, desirous of making display of his proficiency in French, employed the remarkable word '*topjet*' (hardly recognised as standing for '*numéro d'objet*') in the sense of 'catalogue number'; or of the English bard who talks of 'Abdul the Damned'. The veriest tyro in Arabic would know that only God could be spoken of as al-Wahháb, 'the All-Giver', and that 'Abd[1] (servant) must stand before it to make it a possible name for a man—'Abdu'l-Wahháb, 'the Servant of the All-Giver'.[2]

Scholars have occasionally either upbraided Browne for his involvement with the Faith of the Báb and Bahá'u'lláh, or gently shaken their heads. This remark by Sir Denison Ross is in kind vein:

E.G.B. at that time[3] was almost entirely engrossed in research into

[1] It is indeed surprising that notwithstanding centuries of close contact with the world of Islám writers and publicists still quote 'Abdul' as a first name, and whatever comes after 'Abdul' as a man's surname. 'Abdul' can never be the first name or for that matter a surname. It simply means: 'the servant of the . . .' Recently Khán 'Abdu'l-Qayyúm Khán, a noted public figure in Pákistán, was referred to as 'Qayum Khan'. This is not merely jarring to the ears of a devout Muslim, it is blasphemous, because only God can be 'Qayyúm'—Self-Subsistent. (H.M.B.)

[2] M. Phelps, *Abbas Effendi, His Life and Teachings* (New York and London, 1912), Introduction by E. G. Browne, xii–xiv. (There are a few discrepancies between the passages as quoted in Phelps and the actual review in *The Oxford Magazine*, vol. 10, no. 21.)

[3] Mid-nineties. (H.M.B.)

> the origin and history of the Babi religion. It is a matter for regret that he should have devoted so many years to the minutest inquiries into this subject; for he might have been turning his vast knowledge to more useful account. For example, what a fine history of Persia he could have written! It is, of course, true that the rise of the Bab and the persecution of his followers bore a close resemblance to the rise of Christianity, and that they had engrossed the attention of Count Gobineau.[1]

Sir Denison must have expressed some doubt even then,[2] because Browne writes to him,

> As for the future of Babiism, I may very likely be wrong in thinking it may yet make no small stir in the world, but at any rate I am wrong in good company, for I believe M. Renan has expressed the same opinion in *Les Apôtres*. Anyhow its interest to me is quite apart from its success or failure. I think it throws much light on the history of religion, and it is a manifestation of a heroic spirit rare enough in these days. Remember
>
> *How far high failure overleaps the bounds*
> *Of low successes.*[3]

For the sake of historical record it should be stated that the letter in Persian regarding the martyrdom of Áqá Mírzá Ashraf of Ábádih,[4] reproduced in Note Y (pp. 404–6) of the appendices to *A Traveller's Narrative*, headed 'Recent Persecutions', was written to Edward Browne by the father of the present writer; and so was also another letter forming part of the contents of the same Note Y (pp. 410–11). Browne acknowledged this second communication in the letter to his correspondent dated January 1st 1889:

> Thank you very much for the details you gave me about the row about the Bábís at *Shíráz* and *Bushire.* I am very glad that the malice of the mischief-makers recoiled on themselves.

[1] Ross, *Both Ends of the Candle*, p. 54.
[2] Mid-nineties.
[3] Ross, *Both Ends of the Candle*, p. 60.
[4] A town in the province of Fárs.

Chapter VII

The 'Táríkh-i-Jadíd' or 'New History' and the 'Kitáb-i-Nuqṭatu'l-Káf'

We now pass to the next book which Edward Browne compiled on the history of the Faith of the Báb and Bahá'u'lláh. This volume, already referred to in these pages, was the *Táríkh-i-Jadíd* or *The New History of the Báb.*[1] The author of the original history in Persian was Mírzá Ḥusayn, a Bahá'í of Hamadán in western Persia. Browne had been presented with a manuscript copy of this book by the Bahá'ís, while he was in S͟híráz, in the spring of 1888. The diary of the father of the present writer records that the 'Bábí missionary' mentioned by Browne,[2] who provided him with a copy of the *Táríkh-i-Jadíd*, was Ḥájí Mírzá Ḥusayn-i-K͟harṭúmí.[3] The diarist himself paid for its purchase.

Here again Edward Browne prefaced his translation with a long Introduction, and added to it footnotes and appendices of considerable length. This Introduction and these appendices plainly indicate the change that had overtaken Edward Browne's approach and assessment. And in them we come, for the first time, upon the story of a book called the *Nuqṭatu'l-Káf*—The Point of Káf (the letter K). This book was not what it was supposed to be, and what Browne believed it to be. Its story is rather complicated and labyrinthine and tiresome. But explore and probe it we must, because once Edward Browne convinced himself that the *Nuqṭatu'l-Káf* was of supreme importance and unique, his outlook was profoundly affected. On the basis of that conviction he built a monumental and impressive case.

[1] E. G. Browne (ed.), The *Táríkh-i-Jadíd or New History of Mírzá 'Alí Muḥammad the Báb*, by Mírzá Ḥuseyn of Hamadán (Cambridge, 1893). [This would be Táríḵh-i-Jadíd in the system of transliteration used in this book, but Browne's title will be used throughout.]

[2] Browne (ed.), *New History of the Báb*, xliv.

[3] Called K͟harṭúmí, because he was a fellow-prisoner with Ḥájí Mírzá Ḥaydar-'Alí in K͟harṭúm (Khartoum), Súdán. In *A Year Amongst the Persians*, Browne refers to him as Ḥájí Mírzá Ḥasan.

New History *and* Nuqṭatu'l-Káf

During the Easter holidays of 1892, Edward Browne had in his own words 'chanced' on a copy of a book in the Bibliothèque Nationale of Paris, which bore the title of *Nuqṭatu'l-Káf*.[1] This particular copy had at one time belonged to the celebrated French diplomat, theoretician and writer, the Comte de Gobineau, author of the famous work, *Les Religions et les Philosophies dans l'Asie Centrale*, who was posted twice to the Persian capital, as Chargé d'Affaires from 1856 to 1858, and as the Minister Plenipotentiary from 1862 to 1863. Gobineau eventually became a proponent of racialism and Aryan purity, and his theories and writings were used at a later age by deluded men and by vicious men to further their own pernicious ends. But whilst he was in Persia, though disappointed in his infantile racial quest, Gobineau had taken an absorbing interest in the Bábí Faith, and had made a collection of Bábí manuscripts, five of which were purchased after his death by the Bibliothèque Nationale. In addition to his diligent search for the Scriptures and literature of the new Faith, the Comte de Gobineau devoted more than a half of his chief work to the story of the Báb and His followers.

The author of the manuscript, which Browne 'chanced on' in the Bibliothèque Nationale, was said to have been a certain merchant of Káshán, named Ḥájí Mírzá Jání. He had embraced the Faith of the Báb in its early days. When guardsmen were escorting the Báb to a prison-fortress in northwestern Írán, Ḥájí Mírzá Jání had been greatly honoured to receive Him in his own house in Káshán. Eventually the holocaust[2] of the summer of 1852 claimed him a victim.

That Ḥájí Mírzá Jání, the Bábí merchant of Káshán, had written a chronicle or history, complete or fragmentary, has never been in question. But the question has been pertinently asked whether the book which found its way into the possession of the Comte de Gobineau, and which Edward Browne happened to light upon in the National Library of Paris, was the same chronicle. However, the crucial point is not the authorship of *Nuqṭatu'l-Káf*, but the value that Edward Browne attached to it. Was it or was it not a work that merited such high consideration?

[1] There were two copies, one of which was incomplete.

[2] The slaughter of Bábís following the attempt on the life of Náṣiri'd-Dín Sháh by two half-demented youths. See Balyuzi, *Bahá'u'lláh*, pp. 14–15.

There were three Bábís in Ká<u>sh</u>án, who were brothers. One of them was Ḥájí Mírzá Jání, a martyr of the Faith, devout, zealous, a man of the mart, not closed cloisters. The second brother was Ḥájí Muḥammad-Ismá'íl known as <u>Dh</u>abíḥ,[1] who was a staunch follower of Bahá'u'lláh and was mentioned by Him in the Tablet addressed to 'Álí Pá<u>sh</u>á, the Grand Vizier of Turkey, responsible for His fourth exile and incarceration in 'Akká. Ḥájí Muḥammad-Ismá'íl travelled to Adrianople eager to meet his Lord. His arrival coincided with Bahá'u'lláh's harshly-imposed departure. He was heart-broken. But Bahá'u'lláh's instructions reached him to proceed to Gallipoli, where He and His people were to be kept for three nights prior to taking ship for Alexandria. In a public bath in Gallipoli <u>Dh</u>abíḥ attained the presence of Bahá'u'lláh. Thus it was that he was mentioned, and referred to as 'Anís' (the Close Companion), in the *Súriy-i-Ra'ís*, the Tablet addressed to the Grand Vizier of Turkey.

The third of those Bábí brothers of Ká<u>sh</u>án, named Ḥájí Mírzá Aḥmad, was a man vacillating and unstable, who finally attached himself to Ṣubḥ-i-Azal. In Adrianople Bahá'u'lláh revealed a Tablet[2] addressed to him, to call him back to a high destiny. In this Tablet the ringing tone of divine authority is stern, yet the word of counsel is loving and tender. But Ḥájí Mírzá Aḥmad failed to rise to the station to which he was summoned. He and his brother, <u>Dh</u>abíḥ, were not of the same mettle. From Adrianople, Ḥájí Mírzá Aḥmad made his way to Ba<u>gh</u>dád. There he was murdered by an Arab whose name is not recorded, and who in all probability was considered to be a Bahá'í. Bahá'u'lláh was still at Adrianople, and the news of this outrage greatly saddened Him.

Did this Ḥájí Mírzá Aḥmad, involved as he was with the supporters of Ṣubḥ-i-Azal, have a hand in tampering with the text of the fragmentary history written by his martyred brother? One can pose

---

[1] In Bábí-Bahá'í history we come across the name Ismá'íl with which the soubriquet '<u>Dh</u>abíḥ' is associated. Ismá'íl is the same as Ishmael, the son that Abraham had by Hagar. According to the Qur'án it was Ishmael whom Abraham offered to sacrifice—hence the association of the name Ismá'íl with <u>Dh</u>abíḥ which means 'Sacrifice'.

[2] This Epistle of Bahá'u'lláh is known as the Persian Tablet of Aḥmad, to distinguish it from another Tablet revealed in Arabic (also in Adrianople) for another Aḥmad (a native of Yazd), which Bahá'u'lláh has specifically endowed with a particular devotional character.

this question, but to find an answer is well-nigh impossible. No documentary evidence exists.

As already mentioned, no one has ever denied the fact that Ḥájí Mírzá Jání had tried his hand at writing a history of the Faith of the Báb. In a Tablet addressed to the Hands of the Cause,[1] 'Abdu'l-Bahá states:

> The martyr, Ḥájí Mírzá Jání, had written a few chapters, brief and incomplete, on the history of the Faith. These were in the possession of Áqá Muḥammad-Riḍá, the nephew of Dhabíḥ. They were probably in the handwriting of Ḥájí Mírzá Jání himself.

From the *Táríkh-i-Jadíd* (the *New History*), Browne had learned of the existence of a history written by the Káshání merchant. This is what the author of the *Táríkh-i-Jadíd* had written:

> The late Hájí Mírzá Jání, one of the most respected of the inhabitants of Káshán, who was remarkable for his self-devotion, virtue, and purity of heart, who had with his own eyes witnessed all the most important events of the Manifestation, and who for his zeal finally suffered martyrdom (whereof he foretold all the circumstances some while before their occurrence to certain of his acquaintance), wrote a book describing the course of events and setting forth arguments in support of the faith. In this work he recorded all that he was able to ascertain [from first to last, by diligent enquiries most carefully conducted,] about each of the chief disciples and believers.[2]

No effort had been made to conceal the fact that Ḥájí Mírzá Jání had written a history of the Faith; even more, that fact had been proclaimed and stressed.

In the Introduction to his translation of the *Táríkh-i-Jadíd*, Browne related the story of the circumstances which had led its author to undertake the composition of that particular book. Browne had culled that story from a treatise by Mírzá Abu'l-Faḍl of Gulpáygán, entitled *Risáliy-i-Iskandaríyyih* or the Alexandrine

[1] The rank of the Hand of the Cause of God was a high honour conferred by Bahá'u'lláh on a number of His followers. They were distinguished as His lieutenants.

[2] Browne (ed.), *New History of the Báb*, p. 34.

Tract, so called because it was dedicated to Captain (later Major-General) Alexander G. Toumansky of the Russian Artillery, a noted orientalist and the author of several learned works. Toumansky, who also wrote extensively on the Bahá'í Faith, and translated the *Kitáb-i-Aqdas* (the Most Holy Book) of Bahá'u'lláh into Russian, came into contact with the Bahá'ís in the city of 'Ishqábád,[1] in 1890. There he met Mírzá Abu'l-Faḍl, and their acquaintance ripened into friendship. The Alexandrine Tract dealt with certain queries presented by Edward Browne himself, one of which concerned the authorship of the *Táríkh-i-Jadíd.*

It is necessary to stress the standing and stature of Mírzá Abu'l-Faḍl.[2] This eminent scholar was a man of profound erudition, and the range of his learning was vast. Bahá'í history does not record anyone as learned amongst the followers of Bahá'u'lláh. In the cloisters of al-Azhar, the well-famed Theological College of Cairo where Islamic jurisprudence, and Arabic philology and prosody were most authoritatively taught and propounded, Mírzá Abu'l-Faḍl, a migrant from Írán, was an honoured visitant. In Bukhárá he unearthed the only extant manuscript of the *Ḥudúdu'l-'Álam*[3] (The

[1] 'Ishqábád (Askabad) is situated in the present Socialist Soviet Republic of Turkmenistan (Turkamanistán). In those days 'Ishqábád was the home and the refuge of a large, progressive, thriving Bahá'í community. Captain Toumansky gave valuable assistance to this community, particularly when it was engaged in building the first Bahá'í House of Worship (the Mashriqu'l-Adhkár) in the world.

[2] See Plate VII.

[3] The story of this book is strangely involved with the history of the Bahá'í Faith, and a bare outline of it will not be out of place here. For a while Mírzá Abu'l-Faḍl resided in Samarqand, and visited Bukhárá from time to time. Toumansky, eager to find a lost work called *Ulús-i-Arba'ah*, asked Mírzá Abu'l-Faḍl to make a thorough search for it in Bukhárá. In a letter dated October 25th 1892, Mírzá Abu'l-Faḍl informed Toumansky that the search for Ulugh-Big's lost work had been unfruitful, but his efforts had led to the discovery of an old tome that contained four treatises. The *Ḥudúdu'l-'Álam* was bound up with the others in that volume. In 1893 Captain Toumansky visited Bukhárá, and Mírzá Abu'l-Faḍl made a gift of that unique manuscript to him, on condition that it should be published for the benefit of the savants. Although Toumansky wrote a full account of the discovery of the *Ḥudúdu'l-'Álam* for the *Zapiski* of the Russian Oriental Society in 1896 (published 1897), and made available samples of the text and translations of a portion, his other engagements and military duties prevented him from editing and publishing the full text.

In the issue of December 13th 1921 of a Russian paper printed in Paris, an obituary appeared of 'Abdu'l-Bahá, Who had passed away on November 28th. The writer of that article was Professor Vladimir Minorsky, one of the greatest

Regions of the World), a valuable treatise in Persian on geography, composed in A.D. 982. His great work, *Kitábu'l-Fará'id*, which reveals the depth and the breadth of his learning, is not available in an English translation. That book was his shattering answer to Shaykh 'Abdu's-Salám, the Shaykhu'l-Islám[1] of Tiflís,[2] who had written a refutation of the *Kitáb-i-Íqán* (The Book of Certitude). But *The Bahá'í Proofs* (*Ḥujaju'l-Bahíyyih*) and *The Brilliant Proof* (*Burhán-i-Lámi'*) exist in English. The latter in particular, although no longer than a pamphlet, which was penned in answer to the criticisms of a Christian divine,[3] shows the sterling quality of his knowledge and insight.

In his Alexandrine Tract Mírzá Abu'l-Faḍl had clearly stated that the *Táríkh-i-Jadíd*, the *New History* by Mírzá Ḥusayn-i-Hamadání, was based on Ḥájí Mírzá Jání's work.

At the time of writing his *New History* Mírzá Ḥusayn worked in the office of Mánakjí, the Zoroastrian Agent in Ṭihrán. Previous to that he held a post in government service and, according to Mírzá

---

orientalists of his time, and of all time. He had referred to Toumansky's interest in and connections with the Bahá'í Faith. Mme. Toumansky read the article in Istanbul and wrote to Minorsky to give him the news of her husband's death which had occurred on December 1st 1920, and to ask his advice regarding Toumansky's valuable manuscripts, one of which was that unique copy of the *Ḥudúdu'l-'Álam*. Through the good offices of Professor Minorsky that precious manuscript was sent to Leningrad, and the most distinguished of Soviet orientalists, Professor Barthold, prepared an edition for the press, which appeared after his death in August 1931. The English version together with copious notes was the masterly work of Minorsky himself, and was published in 1937 in the Gibb Memorial Series.

[1] The chief divine, particularly in a Sunní community.

[2] Modern Tbilsi.

[3] This divine was the Reverend Peter Z. Easton who, in his own words, had been 'labouring as a missionary since 1873' in the Caucasus and Ádharbáyján in northwest Persia. In 1911 he visited 'Abdu'l-Bahá in London, and then wrote disparagingly about Him and about the Faith of which He was the Exponent. It riled the Reverend Peter Z. Easton that at the Church of St John's, Westminster, Archdeacon Wilberforce had placed the Bishop's chair for 'Abdu'l-Bahá. Such was his reference to Bahá'u'lláh and to the Bahá'í Faith, in the *English Churchman* (September 20th 1911): 'But it may be objected, it is impossible to believe that such a demon in human form could exist, and, even if this were possible, a system so awful, so abominable would find no adherents. To this I reply that this is what has happened over and over and over again in the history of Persia and other Oriental lands.' Next he carried the attack into the magazine, *Evangelical Christendom*. Then it was that Mírzá Abu'l-Faḍl wrote *The Brilliant Proof*.

Abu'l-Faḍl, had been a member of Náṣiri'd-Dín Sháh's retinue when that monarch visited Europe in 1873. At a later date Mírzá Ḥusayn was imprisoned because of his religious affiliation. We learn also from Mírzá Abu'l-Faḍl that Mánakjí was much given to book-collecting, and that he always encouraged and persuaded talented people to write and compose for him. One night at supper Mánakjí turned to Mírzá Ḥusayn and 'begged' him to write a history of the Bábí Faith. We shall take up the rest of the story in Mírzá Abu'l-Faḍl's own words, as put into English by Edward Browne:

> ... Mírzá Ḥuseyn [sic] came to the writer and asked his assistance, saying, 'Since hitherto no full and correct history has been written treating of the events of this Theophany, to collect and compile the various episodes thereof in a fitting manner is a very difficult matter' ...
>
> To this I replied, 'There is in the hands of the Friends a history by the late Hájí Mírzá Jání of Káshán, who was one of the martyrs of Teherán [sic], and one of the best men of that time. But he was a man engaged in business and without skill in historiography, neither did he record the dates of the years and months. At most he, being a God-fearing man, truthfully set down the record of events as he had seen and heard them. Obtain this book, and take the episodes from it, and the dates of the years and months from the *Násikhu't-Tawáríkh*[1] and the appendices of the *Rawẓatu's-Ṣafá*;[2] and, having incorporated these in your rough draft, read over each sheet to His Reverence Hájí Seyyid Jawád of Kerbelá[3] ... for he, from the beginning of the Manifestation of the First Point [*i.e.* the Báb] until the arrival of His Holiness Behá'u'lláh in Acre, accompanied the Friends everywhere in person, and is thoroughly informed and cognizant of all events...'
>
> Then he requested the writer to indite the introductory preface,

[1-2] In conformity with the system of transliteration of oriental terms used in this book, the names of these two works of history written during the reign of Náṣiri'd-Dín Sháh, extremely hostile and even abusive where they deal with the Báb and His people, should appear as such: *Násikhu't-Taváríkh* and *Rawḍatu'ṣ-Ṣafá*.

[3] Ḥájí Siyyid Javád-i-Karbilá'í (or of Karbilá) was a highly-revered Shí'ah divine who believed in the Báb and later became a follower of Bahá'u'lláh. He lived to a very advanced age. Shaykh Aḥmad-i-Rúḥí, as previously mentioned (see p. 20), claimed that Ḥájí Siyyid Javád had been a supporter of Ṣubḥ-i-Azal. (H.M.B.)

and so open for him the path of composition. So I, agreeably to his request, wrote two pages at the beginning of that book, and embellished this introduction with prefatory exhortations and incitements to strive after truth.[1]

Mírzá Abu'l-Faḍl went on to recount that Mírzá Ḥusayn intended to write two volumes, the first on the Dispensation of the Báb, and the second on the Advent of Bahá'u'lláh, but he died in 1881 (or 1882) before he could embark on the second volume. Furthermore, Mírzá Abu'l-Faḍl stated:

> ... Mánakjí would not suffer this history to be finished in the manner which the writer had suggested, but compelled the chronicler to write what he dictated ... first of all the secretary used to read over to him the rough draft which he had made in accordance with his own taste and agreeably to the canons of good style; and then, after Mánakjí had made additions here and excisions there, and had docked and re-arranged the matter, he used to make a fair copy. And since Mánakjí had no great skill or science in the Persian tongue, the style of most of the books and treatises attributed to him is disconnected and broken, good and bad being mingled together. In addition to this defect, ignorant scribes and illiterate writers have, in accordance with their own fancies, so altered the *Táríkh-i-Jadíd* that at the present day every copy of it appears like a defaced portrait or a restored temple, to such a degree that one cannot obtain a correct copy of it, unless it were the author's own transcript; otherwise no copy can be relied upon.[2]

To sum up, Mírzá Abu'l-Faḍl had clearly stated, in his Alexandrine Tract, that Ḥájí Mírzá Jání of Ká<u>sh</u>án had composed a book on the history of the Bábí Faith. No attempt whatsoever had been made to conceal that fact. Even more, Mírzá Abu'l-Faḍl had added this item of information regarding the composition of that history: '... he[Ḥájí Mírzá Jání] came from Káshán to Teherán, and abode in Sháh 'Abdu'l-'Aẓím,[3] where he wrote his history'.[4] Mírzá Abu'l-

[1] Browne (ed.), *New History of the Báb*, xxxviii–xl. [2] *ibid.*, xl–xli.

[3] A few miles to the south of Ṭihrán where the famous Shrine, a place of sanctuary in past times, is situated. (H.M.B.)

[4] Browne (ed.), *New History of the Báb*, xli.

Faḍl had also stated that the *Táríkh-i-Jadíd* of Mírzá Ḥusayn-i-Hamadání, was based on Ḥájí Mírzá Jání's history. He had also pointed out that Mánakjí had shaped Mírzá Ḥusayn's history to his own liking, and copyists had introduced their own embellishments. Inroads of copyists have been the bane of Persian literature. All this indicates that Mírzá Abu'l-Faḍl must have personally seen both the histories. Therefore his pronouncement after the publication of the *Nuqṭatu'l-Káf*, the book discovered by Edward Browne in the Bibliothèque Nationale, carries weight. In a treatise he unhesitantly condemned it as a forgery.

The *Nuqṭatu'l-Káf* appeared in print in 1910—the fifteenth volume of the E. J. W. Gibb Memorial Series, an illustrious library of Arabic and Persian classics. There were two Introductions by Edward Browne, one, much the longer, in Persian, and one in English. The two did not exactly tally. Some seventeen years earlier in his Introduction to the *New History*, Browne had written:

> The history composed by Hájí Mírzá Jání,[1] however, belongs to a different category from the writings[2] which we have hitherto been discussing. Without sharing the sacred character of these, it was incomparably more dangerous to the pretensions and plans of Behá [sic], as any one may see by referring to Appendix II[3] of this volume. Its tone towards all beyond the pale of the Bábí Church, and more especially towards the Sháh of Persia and his government, was irreconcilably hostile. The doctrines set forth in it, though undoubtedly those held by the early Bábís, were eminently calculated to encourage mysticism and metaphysical speculation of the boldest kind, and to maintain in full activity that pantheistic fermentation which Behá was so desirous to check. Worst of all, it supplied the Ezelís [sic] with a most powerful weapon not of defence only, but of attack. And withal it was interesting, profoundly and intensely interesting; the most interesting book, perhaps, in the whole range of Bábí literature. To suppress it and withdraw it from circulation, at any rate while those on whom had

[1] Browne was certain that the *Nuqṭatu'l-Káf* could have had no other author than Ḥájí Mírzá Jání. See *New History of the Báb*, xxxii.

[2] The Writings of the Báb and Bahá'u'lláh. (H.M.B.)

[3] 'On Hájí Mírzá Jání's History, With Especial Reference to the Passages Suppressed or Modified in the Táríkh-i-Jadíd.'

been thrown the glamour of the young Shírází Seer[1] and of the beautiful Ḳurratu'l-'Ayn,[2] the martyred heroine and poetess of Ḳazvín,[3] constituted the majority of the faithful, was almost impossible; to let it continue to circulate in its present form would be disastrous. Only one plan offered any chance of success. Often in the literary history of the East has the disappearance and extinction of works both valuable and of general interest been brought about, either accidentally or intentionally, by the compilation from them of a more concise and popular abridgement which has gradually superseded them. As the Biography of the Prophet Muḥammad composed by Ibn Is-ḥáḳ[4] was superseded by the recension of Ibn Hishám, so should Mírzá Jání's old history of the Báb and his Apostles be superseded by a revised, expurgated, and emended 'NEW HISTORY' (*Táríkh-i-Jadíd*), which, while carefully omitting every fact, doctrine, and expression calculated to injure the policy of Behá, or to give offence to his followers, should preserve, and even supplement with new material derived from fresh sources, the substance of the earlier chronicle.[5]

A chronicle composed by a merchant who was neither a historian, nor a scholar and man of letters, and whose association with the Founder of the Faith was confined to a matter of days, could not be the sole document to preserve a valid doctrine and tradition. Apart from their Scriptures the Bábís had the writings of such outstanding figures of their Faith as Quddús and Vaḥíd to instruct them. It was strange to assume that such a book as the *Nuqṭatu'l-Káf* was the authentic compendium of the hopes and the beliefs, the achievements and the expectations of the Bábí community, and had to be suppressed for ulterior motives. Only two years intervened between the martyrdom of the Báb and the holocaust of 1852 in which Ḥájí Mírzá Jání suffered the same fate as his Master. Less than a decade later the vast majority of the Bábís had turned to Bahá'u'lláh for guidance, although He had not yet declared to them that He was the Promised One of the *Bayán*. Following Bahá'u'lláh's counsel these Bábís had left behind that anarchical state of mind and belief

[1] The Báb.
[2] Qurratu'l-'Ayn, surnamed Ṭáhirih, one of the Letters of the Living.
[3] Qazvín. [4] Ibn Isḥáq.
[5] Browne (ed.), *New History of the Báb*, xxviii–xxix.

which prevailed in the years immediately following the martyrdom of the Báb. What possible effect, then, could the contents of such a book as the *Nuqṭatu'l-Káf* have on the future course of the Faith, that it should have been singled out for suppression?

Let us note the date at which this covert suppression by recasting is supposed to have taken place: at least a quarter of a century later.[1] By then there would have been no need at all for such a stratagem. The Bábí community almost in its entirety had recognised Bahá'u'lláh as the Manifestation of God Whose Advent the Báb had foretold. There was a diminishing minority that had attached itself to Ṣubḥ-i-Azal. Edward Browne had observed this fact, and mentioned it time and time again in his writings. Amongst the small group of Azalís, there were some men of superior talent and noteworthy achievement—men like Shaykh Aḥmad-i-Rúḥí and Mírzá Áqá Khán-i-Kirmání whose careers and tragic end we touched upon in an earlier chapter.[2] Astonishing it is that Shaykh Aḥmad, who was in correspondence with Edward Browne for a number of years, did not provide him with a copy of the *Nuqṭatu'l-Káf*. If anybody could have had a copy of that book and would have carefully preserved it, it would have been that inveterate antagonist of Bahá'u'lláh. He let Browne have a book of which he was the full or part author—the *Hasht Bihisht*. He sent him other material, but not the *Nuqṭatu'l-Káf*. Could it have been that for a highly intelligent man like him the *Nuqṭatu'l-Káf* had little value? Divergences between the *Hasht Bihisht* and the *Nuqṭatu'l-Káf* are very noticeable. There were also a number of Bábís who had refused to give their allegiance either to Bahá'u'lláh or Ṣubḥ-i-Azal. They called themselves Bayánís, after the Book revealed by the Báb. To this day there are remnants of these—passive, aloof and disinterested. They too had no use for the *Nuqṭatu'l-Káf*.

Mírzá Abu'l-Faḍl maintained that the weird title, *Nuqṭatu'l-Káf*,[3] had been selected for a forgery, in order to mislead and to cover up the traces of the author. He pointed to one particularly glaring case of inconsistency: the claim made for Ṣubḥ-i-Azal, which flatly contradicted the thesis of his supporters, as quoted by Edward Browne

[1] The *New History* was composed not earlier than 1877 and not later than 1880.
[2] See pp. 21–3, 28. [3] The Point of Káf (the letter corresponding to K).

in his Introduction. Azalís had always insisted that 'He Whom God shall make manifest' would not appear before the expiration of a long period of time which might extend from 1511 to 2001 years, whereas on page 244 of the *Nuqṭatu'l-Káf* it was emphatically stated, 'By He Whom God shall make manifest to come after Him [the Báb] His Holiness Azal is intended, and none but him, because two Points there cannot be at the same time'.

A look through the contents of the *Nuqṭatu'l-Káf*, even in the résumé given by Browne in Appendix II to the *New History*, reveals confusion of thought and doctrine, incoherence of idea and belief, admixture of tenets and metaphysical speculations. Then the thought forcibly dawns: were the Bábís of the first generation really possessed of such notions? Were divines of the stature of Siyyid Yaḥyáy-i-Dárábí surnamed Vaḥíd, and Mullá Muḥammad-'Alíy-i-Zanjání surnamed Ḥujjat, victims of such hallucinations? Was it for the sake of views and attitudes and trends which the *Nuqṭatu'l-Káf* conveys that apostles of the calibre of Mullá Ḥusayn and Quddús and Ṭáhirih had gladly died? Where in the Writings of the Báb can one find the slightest encouragement to ideas of pantheism? The *Nuqṭatu'l-Káf* is a reflection of the anarchy of the darkest days of the Bábí Faith, and bears the indelible mark of that nihilism which did for a time overtake the community of the Báb.

Edward Browne himself had written that extravagant speculation 'threatened, especially during the two or three years succeeding the Báb's martyrdom (1850–1853), to destroy all order and discipline in the young church by suffering each member to become a law unto himself, and by producing as many "Manifestations" as there were Bábís'.[1] The *Nuqṭatu'l-Káf* is the mirror of that menace.

One can dismiss the *Nuqṭatu'l-Káf* lightly, but not so the two Introductions by Edward Browne. In the first instance there is the question of the authorship of the Introduction in Persian. As mentioned earlier, this Introduction is much longer than the one in English. Since they do not exactly correspond, one cannot be the faithful translation of the other. Was the Persian written by Edward Browne in person, even though it appears over his name? The style does not seem to be his. Some years later another Introduction in

[1] Phelps, *Abbas Effendi*, Introduction by E. G. Browne, xxii.

Persian appeared over his signature in *The Press and Poetry of Modern Persia.*[1] A comparison between the two shows remarkable divergence. Shortly after Browne's death, a long obituary article which appeared in the Berlin magazine *Íránshahr*, a Persian monthly centred in the German capital, carried the statement that the *Nuqṭatu'l-Káf* (although it bears the imprint: 'Edited ... by Edward G. Browne') was not, in fact, edited and prepared for the press by Browne himself, but by a friend of Browne's, who, not wishing for certain reasons to divulge his name, asked that it be published in the name of Edward Browne. Obviously, that unknown editor must have been a Persian scholar. Then, one is tempted to ask: was he not also responsible for the Persian Introduction to the *Nuqṭatu'l-Káf*? The author of that article was no less a person than Mírzá Muḥammad Khán-i-Qazvíní, the celebrated critic and scholar, close friend and colleague of Edward Browne. (See bibliography.) Whatever the case, this Introduction has surprising features.

Whilst proceeding to explain the Sunní theory of Caliphate and the Shí'ite doctrine of the Imámate and the rise of the Shaykhí school in the early part of the 19th century, Browne comments that that particular dissertation is for the benefit of the European reader, because a Muslim, naturally, knows it all. And yet, it is all there in Persian. Of course it is there also in English, but the English Introduction is devoid of a good deal which is included in the Persian. Can one not ask why?

Wherever the material in the two Introductions correspond, there is a tendency to give a sharper edge to the narrative in the Persian version. Comparing the contents of the *Nuqṭatu'l-Káf* and the *New History*, the English Introduction says this of the two accounts of the Badasht Conference:[2]

> ... while the third portion [of the *Nuqṭatu'l-Káf*] ... describing the extraordinary proceedings at Badasht, which seem to have scandalized not only the Muhammadans but even a section of the

[1] E. G. Browne, *The Press and Poetry of Modern Persia*, Cambridge, 1914.

[2] This gathering of the Bábís at the hamlet of Badasht in Khurásán took place in 1848. Bahá'u'lláh, Quddús, and Ṭáhirih were present. The independence of the Bábí Revelation was asserted there, and as a token of that declaration Ṭáhirih discarded her veil. Great agitation followed.

> Bábís . . . including Mullá Ḥusayn of Bushrawayh entitled *Janáb-i-Bábu'l-Báb*, is almost entirely omitted in N.H.[1] Nor is this altogether to be wondered at, for the sermon preached by *Janáb-i-Quddús* on that occasion certainly lends some colour to the accusation made by the Muslims against the Bábís, *viz.* that they advocated communism[2] and community of wives.[3]

The speech attributed to Quddús in the *Nuqṭatu'l-Káf* is by itself a clear reflection of the confused thoughts of the Bábí community in the years immediately following the martyrdom of its Founder. The Persian version of the same remarks[4] reads as such:

> But the third portion . . . which deals with the gathering at Badas͟ht and the strange behaviour and conduct of the Bábís in that locality, which not only aroused the Muslims to fury and clamour, but gained the condemnation of some of the Bábís as well, to the extent that Mullá Ḥusayn, entitled Jináb-i-Bábu'l-Báb, said, 'I shall scourge the participants at Badas͟ht', is entirely omitted from the *New History*. This omission is not very surprising, because the speech made by Jináb-i-Quddús in that gathering decidedly gives some semblance of truth to the accusations that the Muslims bring against the Bábís, of the description that they follow communism,[5] and believe in the sharing of wives and similar doctrines; it indicates that these accusations are not entirely baseless, that is to say, Muslims have not invented all these stories sheerly out of venom, but that there has been something for people to build upon.[6]

In the previous quotation (from the English Introduction) we come upon a strange contradiction. The Bábu'l-Báb, the first believer in the Báb, is mentioned as 'Mullá Ḥusayn of Bushrawayh'. Whereas in a footnote on p. 20 of the Persian Introduction, it is ex-

[1] *New History.* (H.M.B.)

[2] In this context 'communism' should not be equated with Marxism. The practice and the preaching of 'communism' have been attributed to many who lived long before Karl Marx, including the 'heresiarch' Mazdak who appeared in Írán in the 6th century A.D. (H.M.B.)

[3] Browne (ed.), *Nuqṭatu'l-Káf*, English Introduction, xlii.

[4] *ibid.*, Persian Introduction, pp. 61–2. (Translation and transliteration by H.M.B.)

[5] See n. 2 above.

[6] There is no smoke without fire. (H.M.B.)

plained why 'Bushrawayh' is wrong, that it has been perpetrated by those Europeans who had not heard Persians pronounce 'Bushrúyih' (the town), and 'Bushrú'í' (of or from Bushrúyih), and had followed a system of nomenclature that did not apply in their case. It is difficult to explain this contradiction but for the possibility that Edward Browne did not personally write that Persian Introduction.[1]

The pen-portrait of Bahá'u'lláh is there in the Persian Introduction, but truncated, a ghost of the original. Browne's opening words in his Introduction to *A Traveller's Narrative*, as previously noted, were:

> This book is the history of a proscribed and persecuted sect written by one of themselves. After suffering in silence for nigh upon half a century, they at length find voice to tell their tale and offer their apology. Of this voice I am the interpreter.[2]

In the Persian Introduction to the *Nuqṭatu'l-Káf*, it is alleged that 'Abdu'l-Bahá had written *A Traveller's Narrative* to lower the station of the Báb. And in the English Introduction Browne wrote:

> Of this much I am certain, that the more the Bahá'í doctrine spreads, especially outside Persia, and most of all in Europe and America, the more the true history and nature of the original Bábí movement is obscured and distorted.[3]

The passage of time has shown that Browne's prediction was unsound. No better proof can there be than the massive translation of the first volume of the history-chronicle by Mullá Muḥammad-i-Zarandí, entitled Nabíl-i-A'ẓam, accomplished by Shoghi Effendi, the Guardian of the Bahá'í Faith, to which he added copious footnotes and appendices, citing many sources[4] and authorities. The very title that he gave that book—*The Dawn-Breakers*—shows the light in which Bahá'ís view the heroic times of the Báb and His early disciples.

Revealing is this remark in the Persian Introduction, that Browne wrote to his 'Bábí friends' in Írán and Istanbul, to obtain from them

[1] Browne consistently used 'Bushrawayh' or 'Bushraweyh'. See *New History*, p. 32, and *Materials for the Study of the Bábí Religion*, pp. 238–40.

[2] See p. 56, n. 1. [3] *Nuqṭatu'l-Káf*, xxxv.

[4] Including the *Nuqṭatu'l-Káf* (as abridged in the appendices to the *Táríkh-i-Jadíd*).

a copy of the *Nuqṭatu'l-Káf*, and in each case he drew blank. Naturally one takes it that these Bábí friends were of Azalí persuasion. And how was it that even the supporters of Ṣubḥ-i-Azal did not have a copy of this book? Browne's correspondent in Istanbul was Shaykh Aḥmad-i-Rúḥí.

Unless otherwise stated, references and opinions quoted henceforth from the *Nuqṭatu'l-Káf*, are culled from the Persian Introduction which, despite the foregoing indications that he may not have written it, we can only attribute to Edward Browne.

Browne states that the Bahá'ís look upon the Báb as merely the forerunner and herald to Bahá'u'lláh, just as John the Baptist was the forerunner to Jesus Christ. Perhaps the inordinate zeal of a Bahá'í here and a Bahá'í there might have aroused such a suspicion, but there is the testimony of Bahá'u'lláh's *Book of Certitude* which makes it clear that the Báb is regarded as an independent Manifestation of God.

Another amazing conclusion reached by Browne, unruffled by any shadow of doubt, was that the Báb considered the span of time intervening between His Dispensation and the next to be of the same duration that separated one Advent from another in the past. The Writings of the Báb Himself prove that this assumption was unfounded.

One's amazement is further enhanced by the construction which Browne puts upon these words of Bahá'u'lláh in the *Kitáb-i-Íqán*—The Book of Certitude:

> The one object of Our retirement was to avoid becoming a subject of discord among the faithful, a source of disturbance unto Our companions, the means of injury to any soul, or the cause of sorrow to any heart. Beyond these, We cherished no other intention, and apart from them, We had no end in view. And yet, each person schemed after his own desire, and pursued his own idle fancy, until the hour when, from the Mystic Source, there came the summons bidding Us return whence We came. Surrendering Our will to His, We submitted to His injunction.[1]

Browne interprets the 'Mystic Source' from which the 'summons' to

[1] Bahá'u'lláh, *Kitáb-i-Íqán* (London, 1961), p. 160.

return reached Bahá'u'lláh to have been the person of Mírzá Yaḥyá, Ṣubḥ-i-Azal. This is grotesque. Browne wrote:

> Towards the end of the sojourn of these people in Baghdád, according to the author of the *Hasht Bihisht*, gradually signs of innovation and slackness were witnessed in the conduct of Bahá'u'lláh. Some of the veterans amongst the Bábís, such as Mullá Muḥammad-Ja'far-i-Naráqí, Mullá Rajab-'Alíy-i-Qáhir,[1] Ḥájí Siyyid Muḥammad-i-Iṣfahání, Ḥájí Siyyid Javád-i-Karbilá'í, Ḥájí Mírzá Aḥmad-i-Kátib, the chief custodian of Qum,[2] Ḥájí Mírzá Muḥammad-Riḍá and others were disturbed by what they saw, threatened Bahá'u'lláh, and pressed him so hard that he took umbrage, left Baghdád, and lived for nearly two years in the mountains around Sulaymáníyyih. During this period, his dwellings were unknown to the Bábís of Baghdád. When they came to know where he was, Ṣubḥ-i-Azal wrote him a letter and asked him to return to Baghdád. He obeyed and came back.[3]

Bahá'u'lláh arrived at Baghdád from Ṭihrán, on April 8th 1853. He left for Sulaymáníyyih on April 10th 1854, and returned on March 19th 1856. His retirement to the mountainous regions of Kurdistán occurred just a year after His arrival at Baghdád. He went away, unbeknown, because the behaviour and the intrigues of a few men were exposing the remnants of the community of the Báb to fresh dangers. All the available evidence shows that Mírzá Yaḥyá was unable to exercise his authority as the nominal head of that community, that Bahá'u'lláh never acted in his name and by his orders, that the Bábís were not united, contrary to Browne's assertion, in ranging themselves under the leadership of Mírzá Yaḥyá.

The Bábí who sought Bahá'u'lláh out in the mountains of Kurdistán was Shaykh Sulṭán, a learned Arab from Karbilá, who had known Ṭáhirih at the very dawn of the new Revelation. Shaykh Sulṭán, accompanied by a Bábí woodcutter of Arab stock, named Jawád, set out to plead with Bahá'u'lláh at the instance of His eldest Son, barely twelve, of Mírzá Músá (surnamed Kalím—

[1] Qahír. (H.M.B.)

[2] Qum, holy city in Persia, to the south of the capital, where the Shrine of Ma'ṣúmih, the sister of Imám Riḍá, the eighth Imám, is situated.

[3] *Nuqṭatu'l-Káf*, Persian Introduction, pp. 39–40.

the Speaker), His faithful brother, and of those Bábís who realized that only the presence of Bahá'u'lláh in their midst could save them from total disaster. True, Mírzá Yaḥyá had also written to ask Bahá'u'lláh to return, but it was a request, not a 'summons'. The 'Mystic Source' which Bahá'u'lláh mentions in *The Book of Certitude*, from whence the summons came, is obviously the Godhead.

Ṣubḥ-i-Azal wished Bahá'u'lláh to be back in Baghdád, because all round him was disaffection and disorder which he could not control, and he felt desperate. Siyyid Baṣir-i-Hindí, the Indian Bábí, well-famed and well-favoured; Ḥájí Mírzá Músáy-i-Qumí, a highly-learned divine; and Mírzá Asadulláh-i-Dayyán had already repudiated him. The 'Witnesses of the Bayán' whom he himself had appointed could afford him little comfort. One of them was Siyyid Muḥammad-i-Iṣfahání, incapable of aught but intrigue. Another was the same Mullá Muḥammad-Ja'far-i-Naráqí whom the author of the *Hasht Bihisht* has named as one of the admonitors reprimanding Bahá'u'lláh. He and his brother, Mullá Muḥammad-Taqí, a third 'Witness of the Bayán', sons of a celebrated Shí'ah divine, were at loggerheads. When Mírzá Yaḥyá left Baghdád for Constantinople, in Bahá'u'lláh's train, he did not even bother to inform this Mullá Muḥammad-Ja'far of his departure, and his 'Witness' thought that he was still to be found in 'Iráq.

Such was the state of the Bábís that when Bahá'u'lláh looked at the scene, He wrote:

> We found no more than a handful of souls, faint and dispirited, nay utterly lost and dead. The Cause of God had ceased to be on any one's lips, nor was any heart receptive to its message.[1]

To Shaykh Sulṭán who had entreated Him to return He had said:

> But for My recognition of the fact that the blessed Cause of the Primal Point[2] was on the verge of being completely obliterated, and all the sacred blood poured out in the path of God would have been shed in vain, I would in no wise have consented to return to the people of the Bayán, and would have abandoned them to the worship of the idols their imaginations had fashioned.[3]

[1] Cited by Shoghi Effendi, *God Passes By*, p. 125.
[2] Nuqṭiy-i-Úlá—the Báb. [3] Cited *God Passes By*, p. 126.

As they approached Baghdád He told Shaykh Sulṭán that these remaining days were 'the only days of peace and tranquillity' He was ever to experience. Shaykh Sulṭán wrote a memoir of the events that led to Bahá'u'lláh's retirement to the mountains of Kurdistán, and of his own mission to beseech Him to return.

Perhaps it was not possible for Edward Browne to check the accuracy of the statements which he quoted from the *Hasht Bihisht*. But was it wise to present them with an aura of definitiveness? Had he been in a position to verify the stories of the *Hasht Bihisht* he would have found that the list of those veterans who were supposed to have warned Bahá'u'lláh against 'innovation and slackness' was badly compiled. Mullá Muḥammad-Ja'far was pursuing his own ends in Persia; Mullá Rajab-'Alí and Ḥájí Siyyid Muḥammad-i-Iṣfahání were not eminent in the ranks of the Bábís, they are conspicuously absent from the pages of the *Nuqṭatu'l-Káf*; Ḥájí Siyyid Javád-i-Karbilá'í was devoted to Bahá'u'lláh, and even if he were not, he was not the kind of man to throw down a challenge; there was no chief custodian of Qum,[1] there was no Ḥájí Mírzá Aḥmad-i-Kátib, there was no identifiable Ḥájí Mírzá Muḥammad-Riḍá.

As one proceeds with the Persian Introduction to the *Nuqṭatu'l-Káf*, one's amazement deepens. Edward Browne who had seen Bahá'u'lláh in person, who wrote that 'power and authority sat on that ample brow', comes to make the astounding remark that Mírzá Áqá Ján was constantly egging and encouraging Him to assume full authority in the Bábí community, but the biggest obstacle was the presence of veterans amongst the Bábís. Comment is superfluous, except to say that Mírzá Áqá Ján, who came to be known as Khádimu'lláh (the Servant of God), was the personal attendant of Bahá'u'lláh and later His amanuensis as well. At that point of time, he was a young man in his twenties.

There was in Baghdád a Persian of evil repute, named Riḍá Turk. Mírzá Buzurg Khán-i-Qazvíní, the Persian Consul-general, offered him a tempting price to kill Bahá'u'lláh. This man took his chance one day when Bahá'u'lláh was in the bathhouse and His bath-attendant had gone away on an errand. But one look at Bahá'u'lláh

[1] There was a Mírzá Ḥusayn-i-Mutavallí (custodian), a native of Qum, in the fortress of Shaykh Ṭabarsí. He betrayed his fellow-believers.

made him—a man who, according to himself, had never known shame—flinch and turn on his heels. He related his story later, to all and sundry. Such was the power that emanated from Bahá'u'lláh, which Edward Browne had himself witnessed and attested to.

Who, one has to ask, were those veterans amongst the Bábís who would have barred the way to Bahá'u'lláh? Eleven of the eighteen 'Witnesses' appointed by Ṣubḥ-i-Azal chose to follow Bahá'u'lláh. Survivors amongst the Letters of the Living, and the stalwart defenders of Shaykh Ṭabarsí[1] who, under the command of Quddús and Mullá Ḥusayn, held armies at bay, did likewise. These were the veterans of the Faith of the Báb.

The reasons given in the Persian Introduction to the *Nuqṭatu'l-Káf*, for the removal of the 'Bábís' from Baghdád and later from Adrianople, are very curious. In Baghdád, it is stated, daily exchanges took place between the Muslims and the Bábís, and that situation could no longer be tolerated. It is not mentioned that the government of Náṣiri'd-Dín Sháh was aiming at the destruction of Bahá'u'lláh. A state paper[2] which M. Nicolas had sent to Browne in 1902, and was in his possession, was the irrefutable proof. If the intention of the authorities was focused on clearing Baghdád of Bábís, numbers of them would not have been allowed to dwell there after Bahá'u'lláh's departure.

Regarding Bahá'u'lláh's fourth and last banishment to 'Akká, and Ṣubḥ-i-Azal's consignment to Cyprus, that incredible Introduction says:

> The Ottoman Government, noticing once again signs of agitation and disturbance amongst them, and realizing that a schism had occurred in their religion and that the ground was well prepared for clash and dispute, mischief and strife betwixt the two factions, without taking the trouble to investigate and distinguish between

[1] The Shrine of Shaykh Ṭabarsí is situated in the province of Mázindarán. Around it the Bábís, harassed on all sides, built a fortress, and for several months in the course of 1848 and 1849 warded off the attacks of their adversaries. Mullá Ḥusayn was killed in an ambush. The perfidy of the commanders of the army, dispatched by Náṣiri'd-Dín Sháh, sealed the fate of the besieged. They were massacred and Quddús was savagely put to death. A few survived. At Shaykh Ṭabarsí the rank of the Letters of the Living was decimated. Half of them fell there.

[2] See p. 46.

right and wrong in this matter, immediately took steps to send all the Bábís away from Adrianople. . .[1]

Browne had said much the same thing in the Introduction to the *New History*:

> . . . signs of renewed and increased activity amongst them attracted the notice of the Ottoman authorities, who, learning that a schism had divided them into two hostile sections, the one headed by Behá'u'lláh, the other by Ṣubḥ-i-Ezel, packed them off without more ado, and probably without troubling to enquire much into the rights and wrongs of the matter, the former to Acre, the latter to Famagusta in Cyprus.[2]

This does not accord with facts of history. However, one can overlook the faults of the earlier version (in the *New History*), because at that time Browne was obviously handicapped by the meagreness of fact available to him. But the manner of presentation in the later version (in the *Nuqṭatu'l-Káf*) is wide open to censure, and the conclusions the reader is apt to draw from it cannot but be erroneous. Unless the Ottoman authorities were completely unseeing, they could not fail to observe that Ṣubḥ-i-Azal had hardly any supporters in Adrianople. Whereas four Bahá'ís were exiled to Cyprus with Ṣubḥ-i-Azal, there were only two confirmed Azalís, namely Siyyid Muḥammad-i-Iṣfahání and Áqá-Ján Big to send to 'Akká. With Ṣubḥ-i-Azal in Cyprus, apart from his wives and sons and daughters, there was no one that he could count a supporter. With Bahá'u'lláh in the citadel of 'Akká, apart from the immediate members of His family, there were more than fifty devoted followers. How could there have been clashes detrimental to the safety of the Ottoman realms, between Bahá'ís and Azalís in Adrianople?

Thus we reach the story of the murder[3] of three Azalís in 'Akká, previously narrated in these pages (pp. 34–7). Another novelty that we encounter here[4] is the allegation that those responsible for that odious deed were freed from gaol by 'Abdu'l-Bahá's intercession. Then follows a list of the Bábís whom, it is said, the Bahá'ís elimi-

[1] *Nuqṭatu'l-Káf*, Persian Introduction, p. 42.
[2] Browne (ed.), *New History of the Báb*, xx–xxi.
[3] This event occurred some years later.
[4] *Nuqṭatu'l-Káf*, Persian Introduction, p. 42.

nated. Of course the *Hasht Bihisht* is the chief source for the list and the allegation. Long before in an appendix[1] to *A Traveller's Narrative*, these men had featured as victims of Bahá'í malevolence. There the source of information had been mentioned and explained. Here in the Introduction to the *Nuqṭatu'l-Káf*, the accusation takes the guise of proved fact. Equally inadmissible is the assertion that some of them were 'personal friends' of the Báb, and belonged to the first circle of His disciples, the Letters of the Living.

One of the men named is a certain Ḥájí Ibráhím, and another a native of Káshán, called Áqá Abu'l-Qásim. There was a Ḥájí Ibráhím in Adrianople. But his story is different from that which is presented in the Introduction to the *Nuqṭatu'l-Káf*. Here it is said that Ḥájí Ibráhím was a fanatical Bahá'í who, on the boat that took the exiles to the Holy Land, gave a merciless beating to Siyyid Muḥammad-i-Iṣfahání, but later saw the error of his ways and repented, and met his death at the hands of the Bahá'ís. Ustád Muḥammad-'Alí,[2] the barber and bath-attendant, whom Mírzá Yaḥyá attempted to win over to his side and incited to kill Bahá'u'lláh, has recorded the story of Ḥájí Ibráhím in the same fragmentary autobiography where he related his own dealings with Mírzá Yaḥyá. Ḥájí Ibráhím accompanied Bahá'u'lláh, when He departed for Istanbul, without His permission. In Adrianople he attached himself to Ṣubḥ-i-Azal and Siyyid Muḥammad. They entrusted him with letters to take to Persia. He divulged his mission to the Bahá'ís. Bahá'u'lláh told him to do as he was bidden, not to tamper with the letters and to deliver them to the people named by Ṣubḥ-i-Azal. Bahá'u'lláh even gave him the expenses of the journey. But Ḥájí Ibráhím did not go to Persia. He left around the letters which Ṣubḥ-i-Azal had handed to his care, and wandered about in the environs of Adrianople. Later on he went to 'Akká, but not in the company of the exiles. As to Áqá Abu'l-Qásim-i-Káshání, he met his death by drowning, in mysterious circumstances, long before, in the early days of the Baghdád period.

If the Bahá'ís were waging a war of extermination against the partisans of Ṣubḥ-i-Azal, how was it then that the most distinguished veteran, Ḥájí Siyyid Javád-i-Karbilá'í, who, according to the same

[1] Pp. 352–73. [2] See *Bahá'u'lláh* by H. M. Balyuzi, pp. 37–9.

accusers, was a supporter of Ṣubḥ-i-Azal, escaped the clutches of the Bahá'ís? Ḥájí Siyyid Javád, with his background and established position, would have been a more formidable opponent than Ḥájí Ibráhím-i-Káshí. It was tragic that Edward Browne did not detect the essential flaw in the make-up of the *Hasht Bihisht*, and perpetuated its flimsy tales.

Edward Browne next expresses surprise that the Bahá'ís, who believed in the Báb and accepted His divine mandate, could countenance the downfall of a man chosen and exalted by the Báb; how could the 'point of light' turn into 'point of darkness'? Bahá'ís also believe in Jesus Christ and accept His divine mandate. Jesus chose Judas Iscariot to be one of His twelve disciples. And Judas betrayed Him.

The Báb wrote in the *Bayán*: 'Blazes of hell-fire will God transform into light by Him Whom God shall make manifest, and lights shall He transform into blazes of hell-fire by Him'; and also: 'Nothing has the *Bayán* in view, save Him Whom God shall make manifest'.[1]

Then we come once again upon the theme that Bahá'ís had no choice but to obliterate all traces of the *Nuqṭatu'l-Káf*. And let it be said once again, at the risk of boring reiteration, that Bahá'ís had nothing whatsoever to fear from a book of that calibre and status, or indeed from any book, as even the *Bayán* itself had been made dependent by its Author upon the good-pleasure of 'Him Whom God shall manifest'. Edward Browne's argument is extremely weak. The thesis that in order to secure their position, safeguard their Cause, and win adherents, all that Bahá'ís had to do was to destroy copies of a history-chronicle written by a relatively obscure merchant of Káshán, is entirely unmatched by the scale and the gravity of events. In that astonishing Introduction to a book which could not have been the original work of Ḥájí Mírzá Jání, the incredible suggestion is made that the repudiation of the successorship of Ṣubḥ-i-Azal went very much against the grain of the Shí'ahs and their belief in the Imámate. In fact, the very claim of the Báb that He was the Qá'im, the Mihdí (Mahdí) expected by the world of Islám, did not tally with the orthodox belief that the Qá'im was Muḥammad ibn-i-

[1] Translated by H.M.B. from his manuscript copy of the *Bayán*.

Ḥasan al-'Askarí, the twelfth Imám, who in the year A.H. 260, A.D. 874, disappeared from the sight of men at the age of five, and who must return in person to this world, in the fullness of time, to restore justice to it. Furthermore, neither the nomination, nor the leadership or headship of Ṣubḥ-i-Azal could be equated with the Imámate as understood and upheld by the Shí'ahs. The Báb never conferred the authority of an Imám, in the Shí'ah sense of the term, on Ṣubḥ-i-Azal. Other Tablets of the Báb there are addressed to others of His company, prefaced with the opening: 'From God to God'.

It is of little value to dwell too long on all the parallels that Browne draws and the comparisons that he makes between various episodes as presented in the *Táríkh-i-Jadíd* and the *Nuqṭatu'l-Káf*. However, this one quotation from the English Introduction to the *Nuqṭatu'l-Káf* will suffice to show his personal reaction to the two books—antipathy towards the one, sympathy for the other. Ḥájí Mullá Ismá'íl-i-Qumí was one of the Seven Martyrs of Ṭihrán who were put to death four months before the execution of the Báb in Tabríz. Ḥájí Mírzá Siyyid 'Alí, the maternal uncle of the Báb who had stood in *loco parentis* to Him when He was orphaned, was also of that group of seven. Edward Browne after comparing the account of the martyrdom of Ḥájí Mullá Ismá'íl in the two books concludes:

> This is an extremely typical instance of the manner in which the compiler of the *New History* has dealt with the original on which he worked. He adds the stone-throwing of the spectators, suppresses the laughter of the courageous victim, and expands his simple utterance, 'I am a Bábí and I am going to die for you' into the pious harangue just cited. The effect produced by these alterations is easier to appreciate than to describe, but it calls up quite a different picture in the mind, and transforms the exalted and indomitable enthusiasts of the early period into moralizing martyrs conformed to the later Bahá'í ideals.[1]

But the Guardian of the Bahá'í Faith writes in glowing terms of the heroic death of those seven martyrs:

> The defiant answers which they flung at their persecutors; the ecstatic joy which seized them as they drew near the scene of their

[1] *Nuqṭatu'l-Káf*, xlv–xlvi.

death; the jubilant shouts they raised as they faced their executioner; the poignancy of the verses which, in their last moments, some of them recited; the appeals and challenges they addressed to the multitude of onlookers who gazed with stupefaction upon them; the eagerness with which the last three victims strove to precede one another in sealing their faith with their blood; and lastly, the atrocities which a bloodthirsty foe degraded itself by inflicting upon their dead bodies which lay unburied for three days and three nights in the Sabzih-Maydán, during which time thousands of so-called devout Shí'ahs kicked their corpses, spat upon their faces, pelted, cursed, derided, and heaped refuse upon them—these were the chief features of the tragedy of the Seven Martyrs of Ṭihrán, a tragedy which stands out as one of the grimmest scenes witnessed in the course of the early unfoldment of the Faith of Bahá'u'lláh.[1]

Lastly, there is Edward Browne's concern and puzzlement over the events which followed the passing of Bahá'u'lláh—the failure of members of His family to accept the implications of His Will and Testament, and to give their unqualified loyalty and allegiance to 'Abdu'l-Bahá. Mírzá Muḥammad-'Alí, the second surviving son of Bahá'u'lláh, and those who joined him and broke the Covenant which Bahá'u'lláh had firmly established, called themselves the 'Unitarians'. They accused 'Abdu'l-Bahá of having claimed the station of a Manifestation of God for Himself. Edward Browne states that there are now four categories of Bábís:

1. Those who reject both Bahá'u'lláh and Ṣubḥ-i-Azal, very few in number, whom Browne had never met.

2. The Azalís who maintain that Mírzá Yaḥyá, Ṣubḥ-i-Azal, is the legitimate successor to the Báb, and that 'He Whom God shall make manifest' has not appeared. Browne considers that 'These also are few, and their numbers are probably diminishing'.

3. Those Bahá'ís who look to Bahá'u'lláh as 'He Whom God shall make manifest', but refuse the authority of 'Abdu'l-Bahá and follow His brother, Mírzá Muḥammad-'Alí, because, in their view, 'Abdu'l-Bahá has, contrary to the warnings of Bahá'u'lláh, laid a claim to the station of a Manifestation of God.

[1] Shoghi Effendi, *God Passes By*, p. 47.

VII. MÍRZÁ ABU'L-FAḌL OF GULPÁYGÁN

4. (To quote the exact words of Edward Browne) 'Those *Bahá'ís* who, holding that "there is no intermission in the Divine Grace", recognize 'Abdu'l-Bahá's claims (the exact nature of which I cannot confidently define) and regard him as the actual Theophany. These are the majority, and it is curious to observe . . . how in the Bábí church the "stationary" or conservative party seems ever doomed to defeat. Yet 'Abbás Efendi's position was a much more difficult one to maintain than his father's, for while, as we have seen, the Báb's utterances concerning "Him whom God shall manifest" made it almost impossible for his followers to deny the claims of any claimant, Bahá'u'lláh seemed to have left no loop-hole for a new Manifestation in the millennium succeeding his death'.[1] It is evident that in this instance Browne had seen the import of the awesome injunctions of the Báb. After quoting verses from the Writings of Bahá'u'lláh, to bear out a statement which is undeniable that no Manifestation of God was to come for a thousand years, Browne reached the conclusion:

> This last schism, I confess, and the bitterness to which it gave rise, created a very painful impression on my mind, for, as I have repeatedly enquired of my Bahá'í friends, where is the compelling and constraining power which they regard as the essential and incontrovertible sign of the Divine Word, when, in face of such texts as '*Associate with* [*the followers of all*] *religions with spirituality and fragrance*' . . . , they can show such bitter animosity towards those of their own household?[2]

Where could that 'compelling and constraining power' be but in the very shape and ordering and trend of the Bahá'í community. And one should differentiate between animosity and the defence of the integrity of the Faith. It is surprising that Browne did not see clearly that 'Abdu'l-Bahá was not claiming any station other than the Centre of the Covenant of Bahá'u'lláh, and that the Bahá'ís, no matter how exaggerated the language of Bahá'í poets might have been, never believed that 'Abdu'l-Bahá was the inaugurator of a new Theophany. Such a belief would have been blasphemous to their minds.

[1] Browne (ed.), *Nuqṭatu'l-Káf*, English Introduction, xlviii. [2] *ibid.*, xlix.

In 1910 Edward Browne had, as we shall see later, greatly concerned himself with the fate and the future of the Constitutional Movement in Írán. In it he looked for the resurgence of the spirit of the nation. Hence he wrote at the end of that English Introduction to the *Nuqṭatu'l-Káf*:

> Bahá'ism, in my opinion, is too cosmopolitan in its aims to render much direct service to that revival. 'Pride is not for him who loves his country', says Bahá'u'lláh, 'but for him who loves the world'. This is a fine sentiment, but just now it is men who love their country above all else that Persia needs.

However, something of the old admiration lingers, because he continues in this vein:

> Yet the Bábí and Bahá'í movements have at least proved two things, *first*, that the Persians, when deeply stirred by spiritual forces, are capable of the utmost heroism and self-devotion; and *secondly* that Persia is still capable of influencing the world by her thought to a degree equalled by few other countries. For although the Bahá'ís are in the habit of exaggerating the number of converts they have made outside Persia, it is nevertheless a fact that their religion has spread far, both in the East and in the West, and that the number of its adherents, already large, is increasing.[1]

To sum up, there have been two books—one an incomplete history by a devout and courageous merchant who perished in the savage massacre of 1852, the second a distortion ascribed to the same devoted man whose voice had already been silenced when the *Nuqṭatu'l-Káf* was given the stamp of his name. Due to a preconceived idea Edward Browne did not make the right appraisal. Not that it mattered in the long run. The *Nuqṭatu'l-Káf* which was given an honoured place in the galaxy of classics has lost its impact. But very sad it is that Edward Browne could not judge the issue with true discernment.

[1] Browne (ed.), *Nuqṭatu'l-Káf*, English Introduction, lii.

Chapter VIII

Edward Browne, the Orientalist

After the publication of the *Táríkh-i-Jadíd—The New History of the Báb*—Edward Browne was engaged in research of a different kind. He began to delve deeply into Persian literature. And over the course of years he published his monumental work: *A Literary History of Persia*, a venture which was epoch-making in its domain. In spite of recent findings and evaluations, in spite of certain flaws, Browne's encyclopaedic work remains unrivalled and supreme. The first volume appeared in 1902, and the fourth and last volume in 1924.[1]

In the meantime Persia had gone through a relatively peaceful revolution and change of régime. Edward Browne devoted much of his time and energy to the active support of the Constitutionalists and the party of reform. Then there was counter-revolution and a *coup d'état* by the monarch, Muḥammad-'Alí Sháh, which overthrew the Constitution, and restored despotism for a brief period.[2] There was also the Anglo-Russian Agreement of August 31st 1907 which led to the intervention of the Tsarist government and the occupation of Iranian territory by Russian troops. Sir Edward Grey, the British Foreign Secretary, mesmerized by his fear of German expansionism, did no more than present feeble complaints at St Petersburg. Edward Browne helped to form the Persia Committee in London to promote and defend the cause of the Constitution, and his pen was prolific in the service of the same cause. He wrote *A Brief Narrative of Recent Events in Persia* in 1909, *The Persian Revolution of 1905–1909* in 1910, *The Persian Crisis of December 1911*, and *The Reign of Terror at Tabriz: England's Responsibility* in 1912, *The Press and Poetry of Modern Persia* in 1914. He wrote articles for the press, he spoke on platforms, he organised and pro-

[1] Under the title *Persian Literature in Modern Times* (Cambridge, 1924).

[2] June 23rd 1908–July 13th 1909. Muḥammad-'Alí Sháh was defeated and deposed.

vided generous assistance and hospitality to refugees arriving from Persia, he mounted attacks on the Russian government for siding with the reactionaries, and on the Liberal Cabinet in Britain for its close collaboration with Tsarist Russia.

Whilst Edward Granville Browne was deeply committed in the political arena, Bahá'ís eschewed involvement. 'Abdu'l-Bahá had repeatedly counselled them to keep clear of the political struggle, to lend their efforts to the task of reconciliation. There were individual Bahá'ís, the most prominent of whom was the celebrated Ḥájí Shaykhu'r-Ra'ís,[1] who openly supported the constitutional reforms, but as a community they remained free of affiliation. In his book *The Persian Revolution* which was both an apologia for the Constitutionalists and an indictment of those individuals and governments that either stood for reaction or gave it their tacit approval, Edward Browne turned his attention to what he called the 'Attitude of Bahá'ís towards Persian Politics' [Appendix B, note (16)]. First, he cited three different opinions given him by three men well acquainted with the condition of Persia. The testimony of one of them, whom Browne described as a 'brilliant English diplomatist who has generally shewn an unusual understanding of and sympathy with the Persians', was that 'Abdu'l-Bahá had made it incumbent upon the Bahá'ís to avoid political action, '*firstly* because their aims should be wholly spiritual, not political, and *secondly* because their support of the Constitution, if it became known, would tend to prejudice it in the eyes of the orthodox Shí'a, and especially the *mullás*'.[2] Browne presented his second informant as 'a singularly sympathetic and discerning journalist who spent a considerable time in Persia'. In the view of this second informant, 'not only the Constitutional Movement in Persia, but the general awakening of Asia, was the direct outcome of this new spiritual force known as Bábíism or Baháism'. The third person, whose opinion Edward Browne quoted, was 'a captain of the National Volunteers who was a fugitive in England after the *coup d'état* of June, 1908'. This defender of constitutionalism maintained that 'Bahá'ís were opposed to the Constitution, and

[1] Prince Abu'l-Ḥasan Mírzá, the Shaykhu'r-Ra'ís, a member of the ruling dynasty, was a notable divine, highly learned, highly eloquent. He visited 'Abdu'l-Bahá in 'Akká and gave Him his unqualified allegiance.

[2] The clergy.

continued until the end to encourage and support the Sháh', partly because they thought that the monarch would win and also because they hated the Muslim priesthood that had cast its lot with the Constitutionalists. The fact that there were many of the Shí'ah clergy in the reactionary camp, who were bitterly hostile to the Bahá'í Faith, assailed it repeatedly and even engineered to murder the Bahá'ís, the man expressing this view chose to ignore. The supporters of Ṣubḥ-i-Azal gave currency to this accusation, as a Tablet of 'Abdu'l-Bahá quoted by Edward Browne in this connection reveals. It is a Tablet addressed to Ḥájí Mírzá 'Abdu'lláh-i-Ṣaḥiḥ-Furúsh. This is what 'Abdu'l-Bahá said:[1]

> You wrote that it had been stated in the *Ḥablu'l-Matín* published at Rasht that the Bahá'ís were partisans of the Autocracy, and at Zanján had collected aid for the Royalist Cause. One of the 'Friends' must write to some other newspaper, or it must be spread abroad amongst the people, that this is a calumny concerning the Bahá'ís [emanating] from the Yaḥyá'í [*i.e.* Azalí] Bábís, because these people are the enemies of the Bahá'ís. The aim of the Bahá'ís is the reformation of the world, so that amongst all the nations and governments reconciliation may be effected, disputation and conflict may cease, war and bloodshed may be abolished. Therefore they hasten onward with heart and soul, endeavour hard and spend themselves that perchance the Government and the Nation, nay all groups and nations, may be united to one another, and that peace and reconciliation may enter in. Hence they have no part in such quarrels. And a clear proof and conclusive argument as to the falsity of the accuser, which leaves no opening for doubt, is the decree of the *mujtahid*[2] Mullá Ḥasan of Tabríz for the slaughter of the Bahá'ís, and also the slanderous proclamations of the *mujtahid* Mírzá Faḍlu'lláh-i-Núrí[3] and

[1] The translation of 'Abdu'l-Bahá's Tablet is fundamentally Edward Browne's (*The Persian Revolution*, pp. 428–9), but the present writer has made alterations which he has considered to be better expressive of the original.

[2] A divine: applied as an honorific title to those divines that are eminent, and have the authority to interpret. (H.M.B.)

[3] This cleric who, upon the triumph of the Constitutionalists in July 1909, was publicly hanged in Ṭihrán, in his halcyon days ascended the pulpit in the Masjid-i-Sháh (the Royal Mosque) of the capital, produced the *Kitáb-i-Aqdas* (the Most Holy Book)—Bahá'u'lláh's Book of Laws—and read passages therefrom, presaging change of régime and the establishment of constitutional government in

Siyyid 'Alí-Akbar, which were posted on the walls in all the streets and *bázárs* of Ṭihrán. But the Yaḥyá'í [*i.e.* Azalí] Bábís, who are the enemies of the Bahá'ís, and who keep themselves in concealment, tell the Nationalists that the Bahá'ís are the partisans of the Court, while telling the Royalists that they are ready to lay down their lives for the Nation, in order to stir up both sides against the Bahá'ís and make them their enemies, that perchance they may seduce certain souls on either side. This is the truth of the matter; therefore it behoves that men who are just should investigate this very question of the aid said to have been rendered at Zanján. If such a thing had been done by the Bahá'ís, we shall admit and submit. Glory be to God! This is sheer calumny! From the very beginning of the Revolution it was constantly written that the Friends of God should stand aside from this clamour and unrest, this strife and contest, and should seek to reconcile the Government and the Nation, and should spend themselves so that Government and Nation should be harmonized like unto milk and honey, for safety and success are unattainable and impossible without reconciliation. Now when they who wish us ill utter calumnies, the 'Friends' keep silent, wherefore these our foes each day boldly enunciate some new slander.

'Abdu'l-Bahá's counsel was far from ambiguous, and the whole issue was crystal clear. Yet it seems that Edward Browne could not see the question in its true light. The general tenor and tone of this note in the appendices to his book on the Persian Revolution bears out that regrettable fact. As a fervent admirer and supporter of the Constitutional Movement Edward Browne ought also to have realized that the surest way of damning the same movement in the eyes of the public was to associate it in any manner with the Bahá'í community. It would have been stampeded out of existence.

Bahá'u'lláh had expressly foretold the events which shook the power of the Qájárs, and eventually deprived them of the throne. In the *Kitáb-i-Aqdas*, He had thus addressed the capital of Írán, the city in which He was born:

Rejoice with great joy, for God hath made thee 'the Dayspring of

---

Persia, thus laying the movement for the overthrow of absolutism at the door of Bahá'ís.

His Light', inasmuch as within thee was born the Manifestation of His Glory. Be thou glad for this name that hath been conferred upon thee—a name through which the Day Star of grace hath shed its splendour, through which both earth and heaven have been illumined.

Ere long will the state of affairs within thee be changed, and the reins of power fall into the hands of the people. Verily, thy Lord is the All-Knowing. His authority embraceth all things. Rest thou assured in the gracious favour of thy Lord. The eye of His loving-kindness shall everlastingly be directed towards thee.[1]

The *coup d'état* of 1908 staged by the reigning monarch led to the gradual breakdown of law and order throughout Írán, and the victory of nationalist arms in the following year and the deposition of Muḥammad-'Alí Sháh restored neither the authority of the central government nor the shattered economy. Tribal chieftains and brigands roved unimpeded over the countryside and the highways. Adventurers, some bearing the label of reaction and some of reform, were busy in their own ways, furthering their own designs. The preference of the Tsarist government for the deposed Sháh was undisguised and the presence of Russian troops in the northern provinces posed a constant threat to the capital. In 1911, Muḥammad-'Alí Sháh with the support of the Russians made an abortive attempt to regain his lost throne; and the hard-pressed and harassed government in Ṭihrán made a bid to put the country's finances into order. Acting upon the request of his government and the advice of the State Department, the Persian Chargé d'Affaires in Washington, Ali-Kuli Khan, the Nabíli'd-Dawlih, engaged the services of Mr W. Morgan Shuster in the capacity of Treasurer-general. He reached Ṭihrán in May, 1911, with an adequate staff of Americans, backed by an abundance of good will. But the year ended with Shuster dismissed under the duress of a humiliating Russian ultimatum, the second Majlis[2] (National Assembly) which had refused to comply with Russian demands, dissolved and dispersed. The

[1] *Gleanings from the Writings of Bahá'u'lláh* (London, 1949), sect. LVI.

[2] The 2nd Majlis was elected on adult male suffrage, after the restoration of the Constitution in 1909.

New Year Day 1912 witnessed the public hanging of prominent nationalists[1] in Tabríz, by the order of Russian officials. In March Russian guns were trained on Írán's most sacred Shrine—the tomb of Imám Riḍá, the eighth Imám—in Mashhad. The purpose was to dislodge dissidents who had fled to the Shrine. Írán was engulfed in chaos, and during those trying and depressing years Bahá'ís suffered for their Faith, pawns in a game in which they had no part.

In Sárí in Mázindarán, at the very outset of the constitutional struggle, five Bahá'ís were murdered, one of whom, the Mushíru't-Tujjár, was a well-known merchant of that city. They have their niche in history as 'the Five Martyrs'. At Nayríz in the province of Fárs where, in the closing months of the life of the Báb, Siyyid Yaḥyá, Vaḥíd-i-Dárábí, and his fellow-Bábís had heroically withstood the assaults of an army, succumbing finally to the treachery of the foe, scenes were enacted, reminiscent of the earlier tragedy. A certain Shaykh Zakaríyyá, who had carried on a feud with a local magnate, took advantage of the uprising engineered by Siyyid 'Abdu'l-Ḥusayn, a fiery divine of Lár, and appeared, in his name, before Nayríz with a force composed of the discontented. The divine of Lár who had risen to defend the Constitution had little knowledge of what the Constitution meant, but bearing hatred for the Qavámu'l-Mulk, the most powerful grandee of Shíráz, and considering that imperious man to be a reactionary, had sponsored the cause of reform. Strangely enough it included setting up a postal service of his own which must have gladdened the philatelists in later years. Shaykh Zakaríyyá, arriving to lay siege to Nayríz, declared that Siyyid 'Abdu'l-Ḥusayn, the divine of Lár, was the king of Constitutional Government. He was allowed in because resistance was not feasible, and soon, to atone for indiscriminate pillaging, he set about hunting the Bahá'ís. Nineteen of them met their death. The treatment meted to the corpse of a blind man, Mullá 'Abdu'l-Ḥamíd, was shameful. Nayríz had a sizeable Bahá'í community; and men, women and children took to open fields, trudging on and on. Some fell by the roadside. This excerpt from a telegram[2] which they sent to Ṭihrán, speaks for itself:

[1] One of the hanged was Mírzá 'Alí Áqá, the Thiqatu'l-Islám, a learned and notable divine of the Shaykhí school, hostile to the Bahá'ís.

[2] Translated by H.M.B. from copy in his own archives.

His Highness, the Minister of Interior, may our lives be his sacrifice! God is our witness that we had to beg to defray the cost of communication. . . Three months ago it was the craven and appeasing attitude of the Governor-general towards this enemy of religion and state that led to all that pillage and murder. . . Zakaríyyá's threats pour in continuously. Perhaps by the time this telegram arrives the heartless Zakaríyyá may have joined us to previous martyrs. Our attachment to our monarch and our sense of patriotism deter us from seeking the protection of foreigners. O Refuge! O Refuge! Rescue us from malefactors.

At Sírján in the province of Kirmán, the deputy-Governor, who was a reactionary, soon after the *coup d'état* of Muḥammad-'Alí Sháh and the bombardment of the Parliament building in Ṭihrán, ordered the death of Áqá Siyyid Yaḥyá, a local Bahá'í, a man of consequence, highly respected in the town. He was dragged out of his house, and was beaten to death. At Sangsar and Shahmírzád, two areas of the province of Khurásán, where large Bahá'í communities have existed from early years, Rashídu's-Sulṭán, a notorious partisan of the despotic Muḥammad-'Alí Sháh, inflicted grave injuries upon the Bahá'ís.

These incidents do by no means exhaust the long list of the sufferings which Bahá'ís experienced in those unsettled years. They have been particularly detailed here because they illustrate both the condition of the country and the plight of the Bahá'ís. In the writings of Edward Browne that cover the period concerned, the fortunes of Persia are well reflected as they should be, but the afflictions of the Bahá'ís are not recorded.

The trials to which Persia was subjected because of the intrusion of foreign troops, Russian and British (and later on during the World War, Turkish as well), were foretold by 'Abdu'l-Bahá. In the same appendix to *The Persian Revolution,* which we have already quoted, Edward Browne included this extract from a Tablet of 'Abdu'l-Bahá, addressed to a Bahá'í of Ṭihrán, named Muḥammad-'Alí Khán:

As regards what you wrote touching the intervention in the affairs of Persia of the neighbouring States, time upon time it hath been declared by the Pen of the Covenant that the Government (*Daw-*

lat) and the People (*Millat*) should mix together like honey and milk, else the field will be open for the manœuvres of others, and both parties will regret it. But alas! the two parties would not give ear, but have brought matters to this perilous pitch![1]

In London Edward Browne heard those very words from 'Abdu'l-Bahá Himself.

It was in September 1911 that 'Abdu'l-Bahá visited London for the first time, and delivered His first public address to the congregation of the City Temple on the tenth of that month. But Browne did not meet Him on this occasion. In a letter to Browne which is now in the collection preserved in Cambridge University Library,[2] 'Abdu'l-Bahá writes:

> I have received your esteemed letter which gave the tidings of your visit to London. But, alas, the date of your arrival is the fourth of the month [October], and I have to leave for Paris on the morning of the third, because some revered souls have invited me, and I have promised to go, and it is not seemly to break my promise. Therefore I have to leave for Paris, and I go well-pleased with your noble nation. I am grateful for our connections of long standing. Should life be left to us we shall repair the robe rent by separation.[3]

As we shall see later on, according to the evidence provided by Browne himself, he had been for a number of years in correspondence with some of the opponents of 'Abdu'l-Bahá, those men who had violated the Covenant of Bahá'u'lláh.

Fourteen months later in December 1912, 'Abdu'l-Bahá was once again in London, after an eight-months' tour of the United States[4] that took Him from coast to coast. Both then, and later in Paris, Edward Browne together with his wife visited Him. As Mírzá Maḥmúd-i-Zarqání—'Abdu'l-Bahá's secretary in the course of His travels, and the chronicler of those memorable years in the West—has recorded, Browne during his first visit wished to broach the subject of his writings in the past and offer apologies, but 'Abdu'l-Bahá drew away from this topic and said: 'Let us talk of other matters

[1] Browne, *The Persian Revolution*, p. 426. [2] See p. 98, n. 2.
[3] A well-known verse in Persian. [4] He also visited Montreal.

which would be conducive to amity'. Then Browne asked about the state of affairs in Persia and Turkey. Both countries were passing through turbulent times. Northern parts of Persia were in the grip of the Russians, and Turkey had received a shattering defeat at the hands of the Balkan Confederates. 'Abdu'l-Bahá replied:

> I wrote at the very beginning that unless the Government and the Nation be harmonized as milk and honey, prosperity and salvation would be impossible to attain, Persia would be ruined, and in the end the neighbouring states would intervene.

He further said:

> Effort should be exerted to change the character of the Nation, that it may acquire capacity for Constitutional Government and other reforms, otherwise every day fresh troubles will arise, people will become increasingly disheartened, and miseries will multiply.[1]

This was on December 18th. Edward Browne visited 'Abdu'l-Bahá again the next day, and again 'Abdu'l-Bahá drew away from the subject of Browne's writings. A third meeting took place in Paris in the early part of March 1913.

[1] *Kitáb-i-Badáyiu'l-Á͟thár* (Bombay, 1921), vol. II, Mírzá Maḥmúd's diary for December 18th 1912.

Chapter IX

Letters of 'Abdu'l-Bahá to Edward Browne

In the University Library at Cambridge, in the collection of Edward Browne's papers, are a number of Letters written to him by 'Abdu'l-Bahá, over the course of years. Browne listed them in his *Materials for the Study of the Bábí Religion*.[1] They are twelve in number, the first dated August 4th 1890, and the last February 9th 1913.[2]

In the first Letter, a fairly long one, 'Abdu'l-Bahá acknowledges Edward Browne's letter which had borne news of his safe arrival at home. The bonds of amity between them, 'Abdu'l-Bahá writes, are so strong that 'absence is the same as presence', and distance no bar to the hearts. He had always, He says, brought to remembrance 'the days of our consorting'. He expresses the hope that they would meet once again. Time was too short, He states, to explain adequately the principles, the purposes, the conduct of the Faith, but He counts on the perspicacity and the intelligence of that 'spiritual companion' to comprehend the truth of the matter. He advises Browne to aim high and be rid of small nationalism, for whatever is of limited, local consequence is human-bound, and whatever benefits the world of man is celestial. 'Be neither the North Star, nor the Southern Canopus, but be the shining orb in mid-meridian to illumine all regions'. In the field of politics one finds order for the homeland, but 'to take flight into God's skies is reaching for the summit of glory'. Browne must have mentioned the composition of a work of history because 'Abdu'l-Bahá writes:

> You had referred to history; you should so endeavour that in future centuries your history may become the undisputed au-

[1] Pp. 234–5. Browne mentions thirteen Letters, but the one specified as dated April 8th 1891 is not in the collection in the University Library.

[2] The portfolio containing these Letters, amongst Browne's manuscripts, is referred to as F.66.

> thority, nay be considered sacred history, and accepted both by the communities of the people of the Kingdom and by the just amongst the people of the world, because the greatness of this Cause is not as evident as it should be, due to repressive measures repeatedly taken by the Government of Persia, and the severity of assaults, but ere long will its Truth, like unto the luminous sun, be seen and discerned.

'Abdu'l-Bahá ends by expressing His hope to hear regularly from Browne.

Edward Browne answered that Letter on September 11th. He writes:

> In truth I do not know with what tongue to render thanks for this great bounty, and in what words to express the degree of my joy and happiness. Should I consider myself the envy of the world, it would be meet and proper. I made bold to present a letter to Your Eminence. But one cannot regret a boldness which bears such fruit. As long as I live I shall preserve that Tablet, and consider it as one of the most precious treasures.

The second Letter is dated April 3rd 1891, and reads:

> Dear kind friend,
>
> In your letter to my brother, Mírzá Badí'u'lláh, you promised to write us soon a detailed letter. We have waited long and it has not come. It will assuredly come. So intense is the bond linking hearts that by night and by day we look for some news, some token to reach us. We beseech God that such be, by His bounty, the effect of this attachment of hearts, this amity of souls upon the world of existence that lights thereof should, as long as time and space endure, shine bright and clear over the horizon of creation. The heading which you had asked for, is enclosed.
>
> Peace be upon you,
>
> 'Abbás.

The third Letter, dated August 19th 1891, is long and of particular historical interest, since it deals with events that led to the fierce persecution of the Bahá'ís of Yazd. Seven men were put to death in one day by the orders of the Governor, Jalálu'd-Dawlih, a Qájár prince. One of the martyrs was twenty-seven years old, and another eighty-five. On this occasion Bahá'u'lláh revealed a Tablet in which He addressed *The Times* of London, and called upon it to reflect the truth.

'Abdu'l-Bahá in this Letter to Edward Browne unravels the threads of conspiracies which cruelly enmeshed seven innocent men in Yazd. Siyyid Jamálu'd-Dín al-Afghání features in the story, also Mírzá Malkam Khán, the Náẓimu'd-Dawlih,[1] Persian Minister in London from 1872 to November 1889. Mírzá Malkam Khán quarrelled violently with Mírzá 'Alí-Aṣghar Khán, the Amínu's-Sulṭán, Náṣiri'd-Dín Sháh's powerful Ṣadr-i-A'ẓam (Chief Minister), and was dismissed from his post in London. Within months he was editing a liberal paper which he named *Qánún* (Law). This paper was banned in Persia, but copies were smuggled in and passed from hand to hand. In London Malkam Khán had been making inquiries from Browne about the Bahá'ís. And 'Abdu'l-Bahá, as soon as He acknowledges Browne's letter, takes up those strange queries:

> You have mentioned Mírzá Malkam Khán in that he has been enquiring about the conduct and the attitude of these people, although he has full and complete knowledge of the integrity of purpose, the righteousness of aims, the sincerity and rectitude and benevolence towards the entire world that constitute the fundamental and true basis of this community. He has, of course, had an undisclosed objective to pretend ignorance. Glory be to God! strangers from Berlin and England turn into close friends, and acquaintances adopt alien ways.

Then 'Abdu'l-Bahá says that it has become apparent to the generality of Persians that Bahá'ís, notwithstanding all the hostility and oppression which have been their lot, will spend and sacrifice themselves for the well-being of Persia and the Persians. They never re-

[1] This diplomat who was of Armenian stock, and had been honoured also with the title of 'Prince', is a highly controversial figure. Hailed by Edward Browne and many others as one of the Fathers of the Persian Constitution, Malkam Khán has been, in recent years, presented as an adventurer, and even a 'swindler'. Dr Firuz Kazemzadeh of Yale University writes of him: 'His subsequent elevation to the pantheon of Persian constitutionalism is a sad joke' (*Russia and Britain in Persia, 1864–1914*, Yale University Press, New Haven and London, 1968, p. 247). Still it is undeniable that his pen was very influential, and his writings made a remarkable impact. The present writer recalls being given, in his childhood, the writings of Malkam Khán, to study as models of Persian prose.

taliate, but bring balm and peace and friendship. They strive for the common weal. Although blows have rained upon them, they have borne their sufferings with fortitude and patience, and have sought no refuge save God. Praise be to God that in a darkened land they lit a glowing candle, although flames engulfed them.

> In Írán (He says), some are busy with the work of ruination; some others like unto devouring fire, despoil and destroy and disperse; still others, the patriots, are said to be working for reform and reconstruction. If considered justly, it will be seen that these detached souls [Bahá'ís], wronged and patiently suffering, are engaged in establishing, reinforcing and strengthening the very foundation of the Nation and the Government, because the greatness of any government and nation, and the progress and enduring prosperity of any people depend on the improvement of character, the betterment of conduct, the pursuit of knowledge, and evolution in grades of human accomplishment. But alas it is the antagonist who wields the pen...

Next, 'Abdu'l-Bahá states that though in very early days, due to certain circumstances, members of this community took measures to repel assaults and defend themselves, now for forty years they have quietly submitted to their afflictions, and the 'whole land of Írán was drenched with their blood'. Here we come to the central theme: the heart-rending tragedy of Yazd, and its antecedents. 'Abdu'l-Bahá writes:

> For a while past the partisans of Mírzá Malkam Khán in Írán have been eagerly active. And all this while they have been ridiculing and deriding the conduct of the Government. At times by hints and allusions, and in private in plainest terms, they have censured the behaviour of the Prime Minister, and have complained of the disorderliness of government and the thoughtlessness of those who govern. Then the paper, *Qánún*, came in, and Shaykh Jamálu'd-Dín-i-Afghání too, because of his annoyance with the Government, began, here and there, to castigate and reproach it. In the course of conversation, he skilfully prompted and incited the people, and found fault and belittled the Government. It is said that matters reached such a pitch that they wrote leaflets, and threw them about in the streets and bazars. By some

stratagem they contrived a strongly-worded leaflet to reach the Sh̲áh, and since they are aware of the Sh̲áh's disposition, they made great display, arousing suspicion that they have a very large following, and would ere long raise the banner of freedom. The Government prepared to take counter-measures aimed at exterminating them. The supporters of Malkam Kh̲án and Jamálu'd-Dín, in order to frighten, threaten, and greatly alarm the Government thought out a scheme to involve these people,[1] and cause them to stand accused of complicity. To that end they wrote leaflets so worded that alliance with these people should be inferred from them and suspected. In brief, Malkam Kh̲án's brother together with your friend, Mírzáy-i-Hamadání, a few others, and two[2] of these people were arrested. The agents of the Government began, without any proper investigation, to persecute this wronged community, here and there. Whereas, by the majesty of God, those defenceless souls had no knowledge whatsoever of this agitation, neither had they any knowledge of the inciters and the incited. Their course precludes interference with such matters. As soon as the news reached Iṣfahán, because one[3] of the close confidants of Ẓillu's-Sulṭán[4] had also been accused and arrested, the noble Prince, in order to exculpate himself and to veil his own malpractices, considered it judicious to wrong these people, who were guiltless, and make them suffer. Therefore he communicated with Jalálu'd-Dawlih,[5] and instituted severe persecution in the city of Yazd and neighbouring villages.

[1] Bahá'ís.

[2] Ḥájí 'Alí-Akbar-i-Sh̲ahmírzádí, known as Ḥájí Ák̲hund, a Hand of the Cause, and Ḥájí Abu'l-Ḥasan-i-Ardakání, known as Ḥájí Amín. They were arrested in Ṭihrán, removed to Qazvín and imprisoned there. On this occasion Bahá'u'lláh revealed the *Tablet of the World*.

[3] Ḥájí Sayyáḥ-i-Maḥallátí. He went to 'Akká on behalf of Ẓillu's-Sulṭán, but he soon realized that he had gone on a mistaken errand.

[4] Prince Mas'úd Mírzá, the Ẓillu's-Sulṭán, was the eldest son of Náṣiri'd-Dín Sh̲áh, but his mother was not of royal lineage, and he could not succeed to the throne. Being much abler than his half-brother, Muẓaffari'd-Dín Mírzá (later Sh̲áh), this deprivation embittered his life and involved him in a variety of plots, none of which brought him the coveted prize. He was responsible for the death of the two brothers, Mírzá Ḥasan and Mírzá Ḥusayn, prominent merchants of Iṣfahán, now known as Sulṭánu'sh̲-Sh̲uhadá (King of the Martyrs) and Maḥbúbu'sh̲-Sh̲uhadá (Beloved of the Martyrs). When Ẓillu's-Sulṭán met 'Abdu'l-Bahá in Paris, he humbly tried to exonerate himself.

[5] Jalálu'd-Dawlih was a son of Ẓillu's-Sulṭán.

VIII. ‘ABDU’L-BAHÁ

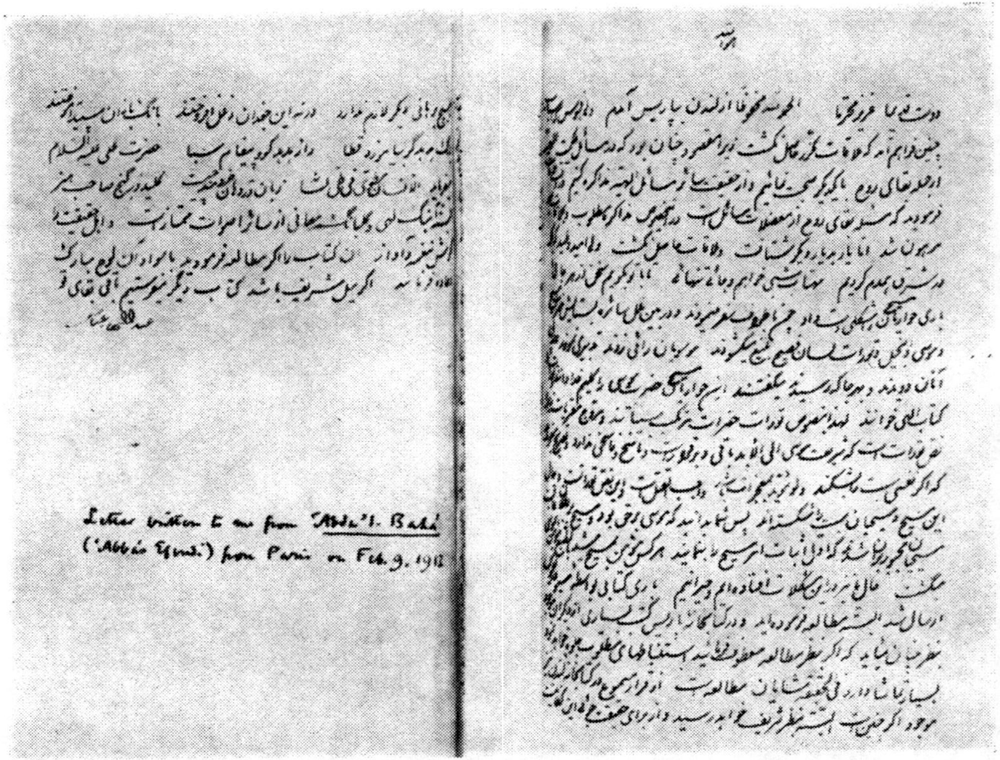

IX. LETTER FROM 'ABDU'L-BAHÁ TO EDWARD BROWNE

Dated February 9th 1913

(by courtesy of the University Library, Cambridge)

Then follow details of brutalities perpetrated: beheadings, hangings, burnings, pillagings, public rejoicings, a thousand fleeing to deserts, numbers perishing of thirst, refusal of food and water to surviving women and children. Relief was provided by Christian merchants travelling through Yazd. 'Abdu'l-Bahá bewails also the heedlessness and the delusion of the oppressor. And after relating the story of a wayward verdict given by a wayward judge of past centuries which resembled the verdict passed on the Bahá'ís, He thus concludes:

> This letter has lengthened, but the All-Knowing God is my Witness, so intense is my attachment to that kind friend[1] that whenever I take up my pen to write, the sweetness of thy memory and thy meeting comes to mind, and I do not want to set down my pen. Thus the chronicle of eagerness becomes long like unto the nights of separation. The rest—wherever thou be, God be thy companion. Peace be upon thee.

The news of the ascension of Bahá'u'lláh was conveyed to Edward Browne by Mírzá Badí'u'lláh, Bahá'u'lláh's third surviving son, in a letter dated June 25th 1892.

The next Letter from 'Abdu'l-Bahá to Edward Browne is dated March 24th 1893, and it reads:

> He is God.
>
> Kind friend,
>
> For long has the road of amity been closed, and the heart and the soul are wearied and sorely afflicted. You have neither remembered these exiles, nor have you consoled these, the desolate, with a letter. What opposition didst thou meet that made thee cut the cords of attachment? It is our earnest hope that the foundation of our friendship is as firm as a mighty stronghold. All the while we have been wondering and waiting. The waves of the sea of amity have rolled once again, and a wave from the world of the heart has swept over the bourne of pen and paper. No longer can I withhold myself. Thy nature and thy character came to mind and I made mention of thy charming self. Just know this, that in this spiritual assemblage your memory burns bright as a candle, and

[1] Edward Browne.

mention of thee blooms in the hearts as a grove and a rose-garden. If you have forgotten us we shall never forget you. We beseech God that in all affairs you shall be the manifestation of His sustaining power, the dawning-place of endless bounty.

Peace be upon you,

'Abbás.

Then eight years intervene. Browne had published the *New History* with an Introduction greatly influenced by the statements and the writings of the supporters of Ṣubḥ-i-Azal. 'Abdu'l-Bahá had met the embattled opposition of the members of the family of Bahá'u'lláh who were leagued with others prominent in the ranks of His followers. And 'Abdu'l-Bahá had triumphed by patience, by forbearance and kindness. Plots were again thickening around 'Abdu'l-Bahá. His opponents, having failed to shake the loyalty of the Bahá'í community, were trying to smear and belittle Him in the eyes of the public, and were laying accusations against Him before the authorities at Istanbul. 'Abdu'l-Bahá wrote to Browne on February 1st 1901:

O revered kind friend,

For a long time no news at all has come from that friend of many years. . . Although the line of amity is unbroken and heartfelt attachment endures, what came to pass that forgetfulness should pervade the heart of friends?. . . We have kept to attachments of old, and God willing shall be steadfast. The passage of time will not bring oblivion and silence. We always remember you and make mention of you, especially when a particular occasion arises . . . because God bestowed a great bounty upon that kind friend. You should appreciate this, that of all the historians of Europe none attained the holy Threshold but you. This bounty was specified unto you. You must indeed cherish this heavenly gift and divine bounty. Although at the present time its significance is not known, in future its import will be established.

O kind friend, know this, that this bounty is a crown generously laid on thy brow, and in the course of centuries it will be the pride and glory of all related to you, all your kinsmen. Do not be surprised. Ponder over earlier centuries. In the days of Christ constant companionship with Him had no importance in the sight of the people, and His loving-kindness and benison had no worth for them. But today, a piece of stone in the neighbourhood of Tiberias is an object of pilgrimage and reverence for half the inhabitants of this earth, because it was once honoured as a seat for His sacred frame. Consider what importance it has gained. It has always been and shall always be so. The Dawning-Places of the Light of God, in their own times, had no importance in the eyes of men and their beneficence was not regarded by the people as a reason for joy and pride. But when the rays of the Sun of Truth suffused all horizons, the monarchs of this world prostrated themselves at the footsteps of these Blessed Beings.

My purpose is to say: preserve this divinely-bestowed gem, and like the hidden pearl place it in the shell of thy heart. Endeavour that this divine pearl, unique as it is, may day by day increase in fairness and fame, and shine with great shining on the diadem of honour in the midmost of the world of existence. . . Should you seek unfading glory and undying sovereignty . . . become the partner of 'Abdu'l-Bahá in servitude to God, to His holy Threshold. . . With utmost humility 'Abdu'l-Bahá prays and entreats that perchance he may succeed in his thraldom before the Throne of God, because the servants of Truth consider total servitude to be their splendorous crown, and service to the friends of God their greatest glory. . . I beseech God to enable this sinful servant, 'Abdu'l-Bahá, to gladden the hearts of friends. For the rest we are always happy remembering you.

Upon you be peace.

That Letter should have clarified the fact that 'Abdu'l-Bahá never did nor would lay claim to a station equivalent to that of His Father, and that the accusations of His opponents were malicious and totally baseless.

The next Letter is dated April 8th 1901. Browne had written on March 4th. It was apparently a reply to 'Abdu'l-Bahá's Letter of February 1st. 'Abdu'l-Bahá, in acknowledging it, says:

From its heading sweet scent arose and brought fragrance to the soul. The heart was made luminous and senses were gladdened, because the context bore the essence of faithfulness, and the tone indicated depths of hidden meaning.

In those early months of 1901, the Boer War was wearily dragging on, and because of it Browne had expressed pain and sorrow. 'Abdu'l-Bahá tells him:

> The captivating and winsome figure of amity and concord will one day appear in the assemblage of the world. All that has been revealed by the Supreme Pen will become evident and come to pass. But the world of man is, as yet, not ready and prepared for such a consummation. This heavenly bestowal will gradually rise over the horizon of man's inner consciousness. . . The suckling child has to be reared for years within the protecting arms of his father before he reaches adulthood. Now it is the very beginning of that resplendent morn. Slowly, like the first streaks of dawn, rays of light will be seen and noticed.

Then 'Abdu'l-Bahá reminds Browne that projects and enterprises which in previous centuries were impossible to realize have now become feasible and easy to undertake, and once again draws his attention to the story of Christ. Cruelly had Christ been treated and low had He been in the estimation of men, and yet how great are the heights which His dominion has attained. Christ was wronged so appallingly and yet He prayed: 'Father, forgive them; for they know not what they do'. Christ was vilified, and His story is enacted once again today. Therefore, they, who today suffer from the same enmities and misrepresentations, only intensify their efforts to serve God and man, and do not allow the tales of detractors to dismay them. 'Abdu'l-Bahá, then, expresses confidence in the perspicacity of men who are just, as Browne would be, to discern that which is true—'they do, of course, sense the blaze of envy and jealousy and feel the glad breath of vivifying breezes that arise from bowers of faithfulness'. Browne's sadness over the Boer War has saddened 'Abdu'l-Bahá. All people of sensibility, He says, are affected by the anguish of war, and it is to be hoped that by the grace of God, in the end, contention will be turned into concord, and joy will prevail.

In the following Letters, two of which are not dated, the activities of a certain Persian journalist in Cairo come under review. In the list, previously cited, Browne gives the dates of the two undated Letters as March 28th 1903 and Christmas 1903. The third Letter bears a date, January 20th 1904, in a different handwriting; whereas Browne mentions June 20th 1904 in his list.

The Persian journalist was Dr Mírzá Muḥammad-Mihdí Khán, the Za'ímu'd-Dawlih, whom we have already met in these pages.[1] He was the author of *Miftáḥu Bábi'l Abwáb*, or the Key to the Gate of Gates, a purported history of the Bábí and Bahá'í Faiths, which was published in Cairo in the autumn of 1903. In two of these three Letters of 'Abdu'l-Bahá the background to the composition of that work is revealed. This is how Browne evaluates the work of Dr Mírzá Muḥammad-Mihdí Khán:

> The author, though a determined antagonist of the Bábís, writes with some appearance of moderation. Though often inaccurate, he adds fresh materials derived orally from his father Muḥammad Taqí, who saw the Báb at Tabríz, and from other eye-witnesses. He also visited Bahá'u'lláh and his sons and followers at 'Akká, and Ṣubḥ-i-Azal at Famagusta in Cyprus, and made a collection of Bábí and Bahá'í books, from which he quotes lengthy extracts in this work, and which he subsequently deposited in the library of the Mosque and University of al-Azhar in Cairo.[2]

Browne himself was in Cairo in the spring of 1903, but he did not travel north to 'Akká. One of the undated Letters of 1903 opens with these words:

> O kind friend of old,
>
> Happy were the days we sat together in fellowship, in amity and affection. The charm of that meeting is still vividly remembered. I hope that at the time opportune the cup of reunion will come round, and the wine of amity will exhilarate the spirit.

The turn of events is conveyed in the next sentence:

> Strangers are on the prowl and rumours are rife.

The intrigues of the violators of the Covenant of Bahá'u'lláh had borne fruit. Their agitation and accusations provoked the Ottoman authorities to take strict measures against 'Abdu'l-Bahá. In August 1902 He was once again confined to the limits of the city-walls of

[1] See p. 29.
[2] Browne, *Materials for the Study of the Bábí Religion*, p. 191.

'Akká. 'Abdu'l-Bahá then entered the most perilous period of His life which lasted until the final overthrow of the despotism of Sulṭan 'Abdu'l-Ḥamíd. Now, 'Abdu'l-Bahá tells Browne that should anyone prominent like him incline towards the Bahá'ís, sinister interpretations are put upon his intention, wrong inferences are made, and fantastic tales are concocted. But, as Browne himself is aware of the fact, Bahá'ís have no ulterior motives. They have no political ambitions. Their concern is with the world of the spirit, their goal the peace and salvation of all. With no one they seek to dispute. Estrangement they hope to see eradicated from the world of man. And these are the closing lines of that Letter:

> Because that dear friend heard and witnessed, drank his fill of bounty from the brimming chalice of Bahá'u'lláh's address and utterance, and was exhilarated thereby, because he became the recipient of honour so great and attained distinction so unique amongst the host of the writers of Europe, these people devoted to God set a very high value on this position, since it is unique and unmatched. Therefore each one of us wishes to converse with that friend of old, to tread the path of affection, to talk of the secrets of our hearts, to seek thy winsome visage.
>
> Upon thee rest praise and felicity.

The other undated Letter (presumably of Christmas 1903) consists in the main of a copy of 'Abdu'l-Bahá's Letter to Dr Mírzá Muḥammad-Mihdí K͟hán, the Za'ímu'd-Dawlih. Probably, a particularly vicious outbreak of persecutions in Yazd and its neighbourhood, which resulted in the death of nearly a hundred Bahá'ís, had prompted Za'ímu'd-Dawlih to write to 'Abdu'l-Bahá. He had referred in a slighting manner to the sufferings of the Bahá'ís. 'Abdu'l-Bahá gently reproves him, and invites him to consider justly the plight of the Bahá'ís, the ruthlessness of their tormentors, the insinuations of their detractors, and their response. He cites the case of Siyyid Jamálu'd-Dín and his endeavours to denigrate the Bahá'ís and their Faith; yet Bahá'ís wished him no harm, and pray for him. Za'ímu'd-Dawlih had asked for some books, and 'Abdu'l-Bahá tells him that for 'reasons well known' He has no access to most of them. He reminds Za'ímu'd-Dawlih that history must reflect

Truth. 'Abdu'l-Bahá reminds him also of the time he spent in 'Akká. Then follows a note addressed to Edward Browne in 'Abdu'l-Bahá's own handwriting, which reads:

He is God.

My kind friend,

Some distinguished people think that by giving currency to tales and legends the Cause of the Bahá'ís can be discredited. Amongst them is this person, who, encouraged by some wealthy Persians in Egypt and hoping for support from known and unknown, has recently devised to write a history in order to cast aspersions on Bahá'ís, introduce such themes that would please the divines in Írán, gladden the hearts of the oppressors, and arouse the intense hostility of the people of this region, that perchance in Syria too, as in Yazd, an assault would be made on these exiles. But he is unmindful of the fact that in regard to earlier centuries—that is concerning Moses, Christ and even Muḥammad—what manner of books and treatises have been written and what calumnies contrived! Christ was particularly made the target of such books. But those treatises became the cause of the exaltation of the Word of God. I wished you to be informed of this reply, and therefore send you a copy confidentially for your perusal. I always remember you and pray for that person [Za'ímu'd-Dawlih] that God may grant him happiness and gratification.

The Letter of January 20th[1] 1904 could be better understood if Browne's letter to 'Abdu'l-Bahá (to which this is the reply) were existent to see what Browne had written to necessitate this answer. 'Abdu'l-Bahá says that He had received Browne's letter that very hour, and was answering it immediately. It is obvious that Browne had felt uneasy and 'Abdu'l-Bahá tells him to read once again His previous Letter to perceive the truth. He repeats the account of Za'ímu'd-Dawlih's intentions and activities. The copy of His Letter to Za'ímu'd-Dawlih was sent to Browne because of His regard for him. No reference had been made to Browne. A friend has been hurt whereas 'Abdu'l-Bahá does not wish to see even strangers hurt. This is the substance of 'Abdu'l-Bahá's Letter.

It seems that correspondence between 'Abdu'l-Bahá and Edward

[1] According to Edward Browne's list, June 20th.

Browne ceased for the next seven years, until 'Abdu'l-Bahá visited London in September 1911.

In March 1906 Mrs Alexander Whyte—wife of a distinguished Minister of the United Free Church of Scotland and mother of Sir Frederick Whyte, Member of Parliament and colonial administrator—visited 'Abdu'l-Bahá in 'Akká, in the company of Mrs Thornburgh-Cropper, the first Bahá'í in the British Isles. That visit lasted only two days and had to be hurriedly terminated due to the oppression of the times, but it evoked from the pen of 'Abdu'l-Bahá, in answer to Mrs Whyte's farewell letter, one of the most remarkable and most famous of His Tablets: the Seven Candles of Unity. To that very brief visit can be traced the notable reception offered to 'Abdu'l-Bahá, seven years later in Edinburgh.

Before accepting the invitation to visit 'Abdu'l-Bahá, Mrs Whyte consulted Edward Browne in Cambridge. His answer was: 'Certainly, do not refuse so great an opportunity.'[1]

'Abdu'l-Bahá reached London on September 4th 1911. Edward Browne must have written immediately, since 'Abdu'l-Bahá's Letter acknowledging his is dated September 7th. It is a short note. 'Abdu'l-Bahá thanks Browne for his kindness, expresses joy at the renewal of an old friendship, and the hope of meeting again. As we have seen, that meeting did not take place until December 1912, when 'Abdu'l-Bahá visited London a second time.

The last Letter of 'Abdu'l-Bahá to Edward Browne was written in Paris on February 9th 1913. He regrets that their meetings in London were not more frequent because they had intended to talk about questions of metaphysics, including survival after death.[2] 'Abdu'l-Bahá hoped that they might meet one day in the East.[3] Then he writes of how the Apostles of Christ fared in their travels and what tactics their adversaries used to discredit them, and says that His situation is similar to theirs. Next, referring to a book which He had sent to Browne in the care of Hippolyte Dreyfus, the distinguished French Bahá'í, 'Abdu'l-Bahá draws Browne's attention

[1] *The Bahá'í World*, vol. IV, 1930–1932 (New York, 1933), p. 396.

[2] Browne had stated more than once in his writings that he had not been able to find what the Bahá'í conception of life after death really was.

[3] Browne visited 'Abdu'l-Bahá in Paris on March 9th 1913. He was given a pamphlet that contained a talk by 'Abdu'l-Bahá on the survival of the soul.

to books by others that can be seen in the Bibliothèque Nationale and the British Museum. He does not indicate Mírzá Yaḥyá, Ṣubḥ-i-Azal by name, but his works are intended. Browne is told that their perusal is sufficient to ascertain truth. No other evidence is needed.

'Abdu'l-Bahá and Edward Browne met for the last time in Paris, and as far as it is known their correspondence ceased.

NOTE

Further search, in the University Library at Cambridge, has brought to light another Letter from 'Abdu'l-Bahá to Edward Browne, which was not listed by him in *Materials for the Study of the Bábí Religion.* This Letter, consisting of three lines, is dated May 10th 1911. In an attached note Browne observes: 'Received from 'Abdu'l-Bahá ('Abbás Efendi), then residing in Paris, on June 8, 1911, through M. Hippolyte Dreyfus'. This is obviously incorrect, because at that date 'Abdu'l-Bahá was still in Egypt. In this short Letter 'Abdu'l-Bahá stated that He had previously sent two treatises to Browne and, although these were unacknowledged, He was also sending copies of a number of letters, betokening His regard and respect. Prior communication, indicated in this Letter, is to my knowledge unrecorded and so far untraced.

September 1974

Chapter X

The Last Book

Now we come to the very last book that Edward Browne wrote or compiled on the Bahá'í Faith: *Materials for the Study of the Bábí Religion*, published by Cambridge University Press in 1918. Even at this late hour Browne was still using, for the most part, the term 'Bábí Religion', whereas much of the material concerned the Faith of Bahá'u'lláh. The less said about this book the better, because it neither adds appreciably to one's knowledge of the Bahá'í Faith, nor does it enhance in any sense the stature of its author. Admittedly it contains some data of particular value. It carries a fairly comprehensive and very useful bibliography. It gives an account of the death and funeral of Mírzá Yaḥyá, Ṣubḥ-i-Azal, which occurred in Famagusta in Cyprus on April 29th 1912. Mírzá Yaḥyá's sad end is recorded by one of his sons, Riḍván-'Alí, who had gone over to the Christian persuasion and adopted the name, 'Constantine the Persian'. He relates that when it came to burial rites:

> ... none were to be found there of witnesses to the *Bayán*,[1] therefore the *Imám-Jum'a*[2] of Famagusta and some others of the doctors of Islám, having uttered [the customary] invocations, placed the body in the coffin and buried it.[3]

So deserted was Ṣubḥ-i-Azal in the evening of his life. To one's mind inevitably come the words of the Prophet Isaiah: 'How art thou fallen from heaven, O Lucifer, son of the morning!'[4]

Almost half of *Materials for the Study of the Bábí Religion* is taken up with sections entitled 'An Epitome of Bábí and Bahá'í history to A.D. 1898, translated from the original Arabic of Mírzá Muḥammad Jawád of Qazwín' and 'Ibráhím George Khayru'lláh and the Bahá'í

[1] *i.e.* Bábís.

[2] 'Imám-i-Jum'ih', a Muslim clerical dignitary, usually associated with the Shí'ah confession. (H.M.B.)

[3] Browne, *Materials for the Study of the Bábí Religion*, p. 312.

[4] Isaiah xiv. 12.

Propaganda in America'. Mírzá Muḥammad-Javád-i-Qazvíní (or 'of Qazvín') was a prominent member of that group of dissidents who, after the ascension of Bahá'u'lláh, broke His Covenant. He had been corresponding with Edward Browne, and his son Mírzá Ghulámu'lláh visited Browne in Cambridge, early in 1901, while on his way to the United States, as stated by Browne himself in this book. Mírzá Ghulámu'lláh wrote to Browne from New York, from Cork and from London; his last letter written from the office of Ḥájí Mírzá Asadu'lláh, a Káshání merchant, trading in Bishopsgate, City of London, is dated November 11th 1902. He states that he is awaiting the arrival of his younger brother Jamál, who is to accompany him to the United States. It is not known whether he met Browne again.

Edward Browne knew beyond any measure of doubt that Bahá'u'lláh had appointed 'Abdu'l-Bahá to be His Successor. He himself stated it categorically in his Introduction to *Abbas Effendi, His Life and Teachings*, by Myron Phelps. At an early date he had received a copy of the Will and Testament left by Bahá'u'lláh. This document is amongst the collection of his papers at the Library of the University of Cambridge (F.66). Of what worth could be a chronicle composed with a very dubious motive? Moreover, Edward Browne had personal knowledge of the stature of 'Abdu'l-Bahá. Furthermore, it was evident by the year 1918 that those who had broken the Covenant of Bahá'u'lláh and had leagued together against 'Abdu'l-Bahá had been repudiated and abandoned by Bahá'ís everywhere. How could vile accusations and dastardly calumnies directed against the person of 'Abdu'l-Bahá, in Mírzá Muḥammad-Javád-i-Qazvíní's chronicle, help any student of the Bábí and the Bahá'í Faith? 'Mírzá Jawád's narrative is valuable,' writes Browne, 'on account of the numerous dates which it gives, and because it comes down to so late a date as March, 1908 (p. 90), while Nabíl's[1] chronological poem (see p. 357) stops short at the end of 1869.'[2] Certainly it is true that a comprehensive history of the Bahá'í Faith was not in circulation and was much to be desired. But a libellous chronicle could not fill that need. Other channels were open and available for obtaining the dates

[1] Mullá Muḥammad-i-Zarandí, surnamed Nabíl-i-A'ẓam. (H.M.B.)
[2] *Materials for the Study of the Bábí Religion*, x.

and the data required by the historian. Do the scholars and students of religion who wish to learn fully of Christ, and the years immediately following His life on this earth, go to the writings of those who cast aspersions upon Him out of sheer venom? And yet Professor Browne translated and published the work of a man who was assailing 'Abdu'l-Bahá's character, driven by palpable hatred. It was done long years after the thorough exposition of the misery of purpose of these men.

The account given here of Ibráhím George Khayru'lláh's teaching in the United States is very curious. The story of Dr Ibráhím Khayru'lláh requires detailed examination. It is another tragic tale in the annals of the Bahá'í Faith—tragic but admonitory. Ibráhím Khayru'lláh was a Christian Arab from a mountain village in the Lebanon. He received his education at the Syrian Protestant College (now the American University of Beirut), and was one of the first medical graduates of that great institution. Eventually he moved to Cairo where he came to know the Bahá'ís. Ḥájí 'Abdu'l-Karím, a merchant originally from Ṭihrán, taught him and helped him to accept the Bahá'í Faith. Khayru'lláh was honoured with a Tablet from Bahá'u'lláh. The harshness of Turkish rule, endemic poverty, and dreams of lands of opportunity had already induced increasing numbers of the peoples of the Levant, in particular Syrian Christians, to turn their faces westwards and go out to seek their fortunes and find freedom in the Americas, notably in the United States. Khayru'lláh's wish to go to America fell into the general pattern, but his desire was to serve the Cause of Bahá'u'lláh, to take its message across the Atlantic, to the New World, to a new clime. Ḥájí 'Abdu'l-Karím encouraged him and helped him. Khayru'lláh wrote and sought 'Abdu'l-Bahá's approval which was given him. He reached the American shore at the close of 1892, the same year that witnessed the ascension of Bahá'u'lláh. At first he took his residence in New York, later moving to Michigan. Then in February 1894 he settled in Chicago. His initial success was formidable. Many embraced the Faith through his assiduous efforts, men and women who served the Cause of Bahá'u'lláh with exemplary devotion over the course of years. Dr Khayru'lláh's work was highly praised. 'Bahá's Peter' and 'the Second Columbus' 'Abdu'l-

Bahá called him. Chicago was not the only arena of his activities. He taught the Faith of Bahá'u'lláh in Kenosha, Kansas City, Philadelphia, Ithaca and New York City as well. Mrs Phoebe Hearst, the wife of Senator George F. Hearst, took a party of American Bahá'ís to 'Akka, to meet 'Abdu'l-Bahá. Amongst them were Dr Khayru'lláh and his wife. This party was further augmented in Paris and in Cairo, and finally totalled fifteen. They divided into three groups, and the first reached 'Akká on December 10th 1898. 'Abdu'l-Bahá accorded Ibráhím Khayru'lláh a signal honour by choosing him to be His companion when He laid the foundation-stone of the Shrine of the Báb on Mount Carmel.

But Ibráhím Khayru'lláh became ambitious, dreamt of power, introduced his own contrived doctrines, sought leadership and a position of authority. Let 'Abdu'l-Bahá be concerned with the East, his inflated ego prompted; he, Ibráhím Khayru'lláh, the successful missioner, would have the West to direct. However he soon saw that 'Abdu'l-Bahá, in spite of having graciously and generously recognised the worth of his endeavour, would never countenance such a grave deviation, and so he went over to the camp of the breakers of the Covenant that had at its head no less a person than Mírzá Muḥammad-'Alí, the second surviving son of Bahá'u'lláh. Letters written by him to Browne which the latter quotes and refers to in this book, as well as the narrative of Muḥammad-Javád-i-Qazvíní, bear out the fact that Dr Khayru'lláh had grievously broken faith. 'Abdu'l-Bahá made several attempts to save him from his aberrations. Ḥájí 'Abdu'l Karím-i-Ṭihrání, who had done much for him in the past, went to America on 'Abdu'l-Bahá's instruction to help Khayru'lláh see how abominably he had erred. He was at the same time to explain the situation to the American Bahá'í community. There is a statement in the book we are now considering that schism had already taken place. This was not so.

Mírzá Muḥammad-'Alí sent his son, Mírzá Shu'áu'lláh, to give support to Ibráhím Khayru'lláh. At a later date, as mentioned before, Mírzá Ghulámu'lláh, the son of Muḥammad-Javád-i-Qazvíní, also went to his aid. But all this marshalling of forces was of no avail. No breach was effected in the ranks of the American Bahá'ís. There were a few who were bewildered, but none to take up cudgels on behalf of Dr Khayru'lláh. Another Bahá'í, resident in Cairo, Ḥájí Mírzá Ḥasan-i-Khurásání, followed up the visit of the Ṭihrání merchant. He too made every effort to rescue Khayru'lláh. But these efforts were also of no avail. Subsequent to the storm and stress of Khayru'lláh's defection which, however testing, had not broken the American Bahá'í community, the great scholar and teacher, Mírzá Abu'l-Faḍl of Gulpáygán, spent a year in the United States from 1901 to 1902.

Edward Browne devoted many pages of *Materials for the Study of the Bábí Religion* to reports of Ibráhím Khayru'lláh's lessons in teaching the Faith and his teaching methods, sent to him by a Miss A. H. of Brooklyn, N.Y., in addition to a lengthy account of Dr Khayru'lláh's defection. The conclusion could be no other than that the Bahá'í teachings presented to the Americans were a hotch-potch of half-truths, weird notions, jumbled mysticism, and laughable exaggeration. The time did certainly come when Dr Khayru'lláh gave free rein to his imagination. But it was not on the foundation of Khayru'lláh's distortions that the faith of the American Bahá'ís rested. The faithfulness, the writings, the very lives of those early Bahá'ís of the United States attest to this. The mass of nonsense reported by the unnamed American lady brings to mind some of the nightmarish doctrines presented in the *Nuqṭatu'l-Káf*.

In the excellent bibliography provided in this book, Browne listed such expositions of the Faith and its teachings as *Some Answered Questions*—'Abdu'l-Bahá's Table Talks in 'Akká compiled by Laura Clifford Barney (later Mme Dreyfus-Barney), and works by the erudite French Bahá'í, Hippolyte Dreyfus. Hardly any indication can be found of the contents of these books and others available in Western languages. But the most glaring omission is the absence of adequate reference to the historic and epoch-making travels of 'Abdu'l-Bahá in the Western world. There is a derogatory remark in this connection in Khayru'lláh's last letter to Browne, dated April 4th 1917, which is quoted in full. And there are cursory references in the bibliography. These constitute the sum total of what is offered in this book regarding 'Abdu'l-Bahá's visit to Europe and North America. Surely the reception accorded to 'Abdu'l-Bahá in the capitals and major cities of the West, the throng of people from all ranks of life to the presence of 'Abdu'l-Bahá in these main centres of population, witnessed by Edward Browne himself in London and Paris, the talks which 'Abdu'l-Bahá delivered in all varieties of congregations, societies, assemblages and gatherings as reported in scores of newspapers and periodicals, furnished valuable material for the study of the Bahá'í Faith. But these are conspicuously absent from Edward Browne's last work on the Faith of the Báb and Bahá'u'lláh.

Chapter XI

Closing Years

The contrast that one finds between what Edward Browne wrote in the early days and what he wrote in 1917 is strange and compelling.

> The spirit which pervades the Bábís[1] is such that it can hardly fail to affect most powerfully all subjected to its influence. It may appal or attract: it cannot be ignored or disregarded. Let those who have not seen disbelieve me if they will; but, should that spirit once reveal itself to them, they will experience an emotion which they are not likely to forget.

This he recorded in 1891 in his Introduction to *A Traveller's Narrative* (xxxix). In 1893 he wrote in *A Year Amongst the Persians:*

> The memory of those assemblies[2] can never fade from my mind; the recollection of those faces and those tones no time can efface. I have gazed with awe on the workings of a mighty Spirit,[3] and I marvel whereunto it tends. O people of the Báb! sorely persecuted, compelled to silence, but steadfast now as at Sheykh Ṭabarsí and Zanján, what destiny is concealed for you behind the veil of the Future?[4]

And when Browne came to compose his *Materials for the Study of the Bábí Religion*, the Faith of Bahá'u'lláh had achieved triumphs undreamed of in the last decade of the nineteenth century. Now he could meet and converse with Bahá'ís of his own nation, and at his own doorstep. But gone is that vivid appreciation and keen foresight which informed his writings of an earlier epoch. Instead, these are the words which conclude his Introduction to his last work:

> Of the future of Bahá'ism it is difficult to hazard a conjecture,

[1] By the Bábís he meant the Bahá'ís, as he was writing these lines in connection with his visit to Bahjí, 'Akká.

[2] Meetings with the Bahá'ís, particularly in S͟híráz. (H.M.B.)

[3] This was the Spirit emanating from Bahá'u'lláh. (H.M.B.)

[4] Browne, *A Year Amongst the Persians* (1926), p. 325.

especially at the present time,[1] when we are more cut off from any trustworthy knowledge of what is happening in the world than at any previous period for many centuries. Less than a month ago[2] the centenary of Bahá'u'lláh's birth was celebrated in America, whither his teachings have spread only within the last twenty years, but what influence they have attained or may in the future attain there or elsewhere it is impossible to conjecture.[3]

Only two months later,[4] Professor Browne was reading a paper before the British Academy (of which he was a Fellow), and there he said

> that Persia gave birth to one of the oldest religions, Zoroastrianism, and one of the most modern, Bábíism or Bahá'ism [sic]. . . The latter . . . has not only spread widely in Asia beyond the Persian frontiers, but has had during the last eighteen years a very remarkable success in America. . .[5]

A change of emphasis is very noticeable.

'Abdu'l-Bahá passed away on November 28th 1921. Browne was moved to write this of Him in the January 1922 issue of the *Journal of the Royal Asiatic Society:*

> The death of 'Abbás Efendi, better known since he succeeded his father, Bahá'u'lláh, thirty years ago as 'Abdu'l-Bahá, deprives Persia of one of the most notable of her children and the East of a remarkable personality, who has probably exercised a greater influence not only in the Orient but in the Occident than any Asiatic thinker and teacher of recent times. The best account of him in English is that published in 1903 by G. P. Putnam's Sons under the title of the *Life and Teachings of Abbas Effendi*, compiled by Myron H. Phelps chiefly from information supplied by Bahiyya Khánam.[6] She states that her brother's birth almost coincided with the 'Manifestation' of Mírzá 'Alí Muḥammad, the Báb

[1] This refers to the Great War.
[2] These words were written December 10th 1917.
[3] Browne, *Materials for the Study of the Bábí Religion*, xxiv.
[4] February 6th 1918.
[5] That paper was published as *The Persian Constitutional Movement* (London, 1918). The quotation occurs on p. 5.
[6] Bahíyyih Khánum, sister of 'Abdu'l-Bahá.

(24th May, 1844),[1] and that she was his junior by three years. Both dates are put three years earlier by another reputable authority,[2] but in any case both brother and sister were mere children when, after the great persecution of the Bábís in 1852, their father Bahá'u'lláh and his family were exiled from Persia, first to Baghdád (1852–63), then to Adrianople (1863–8), and lastly to 'Akká (St. Jean d'Acre) in Syria, where Bahá'u'lláh died on 28th May,[3] 1892, and which his son 'Abdu'l-Bahá was only permitted to leave at will after the Turkish Revolution in 1908. Subsequently to that date he undertook several extensive journeys in Europe and America, visiting London and Paris in 1911, America in 1912, Budapest in 1913, and Paris, Stuttgart, Vienna, and Budapest in the early summer of 1914.[4] In all these countries he had followers, but chiefly in America, where an active propaganda had been carried on since 1893 with very considerable success, resulting in the formation of important Bahá'í centres in New York, Chicago, San Francisco, and other cities. One of the most notable practical results of the Bahá'í ethical teaching in the United States has been, according to the recent testimony of an impartial and qualified observer, the establishment in Bahá'í circles in New York of a real fraternity between black and white, and an unprecedented lifting of the 'colour bar', described by the said observer as 'almost miraculous'.

Ample materials exist even in English for the study of the remarkable personality who has now passed from our midst and of the doctrines he taught; and especially authoritative are the works of M. Hippolyte Dreyfus and his wife (formerly Miss Laura Clifford Barney), who combine intimacy and sympathy with their hero with sound knowledge and wide experience. In their works and in that of Mr. Myron H. Phelps must be sought those par-

[1] 'Abdu'l-Bahá was born on May 23rd 1844. (H.M.B.)

[2] See E. G. Browne's *Materials for the Study of the Bábí Religion* (Cambridge, 1918, pp. 320–1). (E.G.B.)

[3] The correct date is May 29th.

[4] These dates are not exactly correct. 'Abdu'l-Bahá, returning from the United States, visited Britain once again (December 13th 1912–January 21st 1913). Thence He proceeded to Paris. Visits to Central Europe were made in the spring and early summer of 1913. He left France for Egypt on June 12th 1913 and reached Port Said on the 17th. The rest of the year, He was mostly in Alexandria, and returned to the Holy Land in the early part of December.

ticulars which it is impossible to include in this brief obituary notice.

Once again a change is noticeable and once again there is warmth of feeling. Recognition is given to the spiritual power possessed by 'Abdu'l-Bahá. His vast influence springing from that spiritual power is admitted. Within the compass of a short obituary article adequate reference is made to His historic journeys. In contrast to the sterile tones of the book of four years before, the salubrious and healing effects of the spread of Bahá'í teachings are emphasized. Readers are told to seek information in works of those who were adherents of 'Abdu'l-Bahá or his admirer.

After the publication of the final volume of his *Literary History of Persia* in 1924, in which there are copious references to the Bábí and the Bahá'í Faith, Browne suffered a severe heart attack. For eight months he was devotedly tended by his wife, but she died in June 1925, and he never recovered from the sorrow and the pain of his bereavement. The end came in Cambridge on January 5th 1926, and he was laid to rest beside his wife at Elswick Cemetery, Newcastle-on-Tyne.

So closed the career of this eminent orientalist, matchless amongst his peers for his knowledge of Persia and Persian, a man of great charm and great learning, who wielded an able and fluent pen, and produced both excellent verse and excellent prose.

No Western scholar has ever equalled the effort of Edward Granville Browne in seeking and preserving for generations to come the story of the birth and the rise of a Faith which was destined, as he foresaw at the onset of his distinguished career, to have a significance comparable to that of the other great religions of the world. The Comte de Gobineau's classical work was gathering dust when Edward Browne took up his pen to write of a dawning Faith with zest and admiration. Many, there must have been, particularly in academic circles, on both sides of the Atlantic, who made their first acquaintance with that thrilling story in the writings of Edward Browne.

Bahá'ís undoubtedly owe to Edward Granville Browne a deep

debt of gratitude. He gave to posterity the only pen-portrait of Bahá'u'lláh, majestic and awe-inspiring. He wrote an obituary note on the passing of 'Abdu'l-Bahá, which was just and noble and true. Despite some mistaken views, his well-merited fame is enduring.

And the import of Edward Browne's visit to 'Akká, leading as it did to four interviews accorded to him by Bahá'u'lláh, cannot be overstressed. The pen-portrait, unique in the records of mankind, took shape from that visit. Furthermore, such was 'Abdu'l-Bahá's estimation of that event that He told Edward Browne, in later years: 'God bestowed a great bounty upon that kind friend. You should appreciate this, that of all the historians of Europe none attained the holy Threshold but you. This bounty was specified unto you.' At the close of the first Bahá'í century, the Guardian of the Bahá'í Faith wrote that those unparalleled interviews were 'immortalized by the Exile's historic declaration that "these fruitless strifes, these ruinous wars shall pass away and the 'Most Great Peace' shall come."'

Bibliography

AVERY, P. *Modern Iran*. Rev. ed. London: Ernest Benn Limited, 1967.

Bahá'í Revelation, The. A Selection from the Bahá'í Holy Writings. London: Bahá'í Publishing Trust, 1955.

Bahá'í World, The. An International Record. April 1930–1932. Vol. IV. New York: Bahá'í Publishing Committee, 1933.

BAHÁ'U'LLÁH. *Epistle to the Son of the Wolf*. Trans. by Shoghi Effendi. Wilmette, Illinois: Bahá'í Publishing Committee, 1941.

—— *Gleanings from the Writings of Bahá'u'lláh*. Trans. by Shoghi Effendi. London: Bahá'í Publishing Trust, 1949.

—— *The Kitáb-i-Íqán. The Book of Certitude*. Trans. by Shoghi Effendi. London: Bahá'í Publishing Trust. 2nd ed. 1961.

—— 'Tablet of Ṭarázát', in *The Bahá'í Revelation*. A Selection from the Bahá'í Holy Writings. London: Bahá'í Publishing Trust, 1955.

BALYUZI, H. M. *Bahá'u'lláh*. London: George Ronald, 1963. Repr. 1968.

BROWNE, E. G. (in order of publication)

—— 'The Bábís of Persia. I. Sketch of their History, and Personal Experiences amongst them. II. Their Literature and Doctrines'. *The Journal of the Royal Asiatic Society of Great Britain and Ireland*, vol. XXI, July and October, 1889.

—— (ed.) *A Traveller's Narrative written to illustrate the Episode of the Báb*. Edited in the original Persian, and translated into English, with an Introduction and Explanatory Notes. Vol. I, Persian Text. Vol. II, English Translation and Notes. Cambridge University Press, 1891.

—— 'Catalogue and Description of 27 Bábí Manuscripts'. *Journal of the Royal Asiatic Society*, vol. XXIV, July and October, 1892.

—— *A Year Amongst the Persians:* Impressions as to the Life, Character and Thought of the People of Persia, received during twelve months' residence in that country in the years 1887–8. London: A. & C. Black, 1893. 2nd ed. Cambridge University Press, 1926. 3rd ed. London: A. & C. Black, 1959.

Browne, E. G. (*cont.*)

—— (ed.) *The Táríkh-i-Jadíd or New History of Mírzá 'Alí Muḥammad the Báb*, by Mírzá Ḥuseyn of Hamadán, translated from the Persian, with an Introduction, Illustrations, and Appendices. Cambridge University Press, 1893.

—— 'Personal Reminiscences of the Bābī Insurrection at Zanjān in 1850, written in Persian by Āqā 'Abdu'l-Aḥad-i-Zanjānī, and translated into English'. *Journal of the Royal Asiatic Society*, vol. xxix, October, 1897.

—— *A Literary History of Persia From Firdawsí to Sa'dí*. London: T. Fisher Unwin, 1906.

—— (ed.) *Kitáb-i-Nuqṭatu'l-Káf*, being the earliest History of the Bábís compiled by Ḥájji Mírzá Jání of Káshán between the years A.D. 1850 and 1852, edited from the unique Paris Ms. suppl. Persan 1071. E. J. W. Gibb Memorial, vol. xv. Leyden: E. J. Brill; and London: Luzac & Co., 1910.

—— *The Persian Revolution of 1905–1909*. Cambridge University Press, 1910.

—— *The Press and Poetry of Modern Persia*. Partly based on the Manuscript Work of Mírzá Muḥammad 'Alí Khán 'Tarbiyat' of Tabríz. Cambridge University Press, 1914.

—— (ed.) *Materials for the Study of the Bábí Religion*, compiled by Edward G. Browne. Cambridge University Press, 1918.

—— *The Persian Constitutional Movement*. (From the Proc. of the British Academy, vol. 8.) London (Oxf.): Oxford University Press, 1918.

—— 'Sir 'Abdu'l-Baha 'Abbas'. *Journal of the Royal Asiatic Society*, n.s., January, 1922.

Curzon, G. N. *Persia and the Persian Question*. London: Longmans, Green and Co., 1892.

Jackson, S. *The Sassoons*. Repr. London: William Heinemann Ltd, 1968.

Kamshad, H. *Modern Persian Prose Literature*. Cambridge University Press, 1966.

Kazemzadeh, F. *Russia and Britain in Persia, 1864–1914*. New Haven and London: Yale University Press, 1968.

Lytton, N. A. S. *Wilfrid Scawen Blunt, A Memoir*. London: Macdonald & Co. (Publishers), Ltd, 1961.

MARLOWE, J. *Iran (A Short Political Guide)*. London and Dunmow: Pall Mall Press, 1963.

MONTAGU, E. S. *An Indian Diary*. Ed. by V. Montagu. London: William Heinemann Ltd, 1930.

NABÍL-I-A'ẒAM (Muḥammad-i-Zarandí). *The Dawn-Breakers*. Nabíl's Narrative of the Early Days of the Bahá'í Revelation. Wilmette, Illinois: Bahá'í Publishing Trust, 1932. Repr. 1953.

NICOLAS, A.-L.-M. *Seyyèd Ali Mohammed dit le Bâb*. Paris: Dujarric & Cie., 1905.

PHELPS, M. H. *Life and Teachings of Abbas Effendi*. With an introduction by Edward Granville Browne. 2nd ed. rev. New York: G. P. Putnam's Sons, 1912.

QAZVÍNÍ, MÍRZÁ MUḤAMMAD KHÁN. *Bíst Maqálih* (Twenty Essays). Ṭihrán: Ibn-i-Síná & Adab, 1332 (1953).

ROSS, E. D. *Both Ends of the Candle*. London: Faber and Faber Limited, 1943.

RYPKA, J. *History of Iranian Literature*. Written in collaboration with Otakar Klíma, Věra Kubíčková, Felix Tauer, Jiří Bečka, Jiří Cejpek, Jan Marek, I. Hrbek and J. T. P. De Bruijn. Ed. by Karl Jahn. Dordrecht-Holland: D. Reidel Publishing Company, 1968.

SHOGHI EFFENDI. *The Dispensation of Bahá'u'lláh*. London: Bahá'í Publishing Trust, 1947.

—— *God Passes By*. Wilmette, Illinois: Bahá'í Publishing Trust, 1944. 5th repr. 1965.

UPTON, J. M. *The History of Modern Iran, An Interpretation*. Harvard Middle Eastern Monographs II. Cambridge, Massachusetts: Harvard University Press, 1960.

WILBER, D. N. *Iran, Past and Present*. 6th ed. Princeton, New Jersey: Princeton University Press, 1967.

Index

Titles of books, periodicals, and Tablets are italicized. Footnotes are indicated by the abbreviation n. after the page number; if the name or subject occurs both in the text and in a note, this is indicated by 'p. — and n.'. Principal themes are shown by bold figures.

Index

Abu'l-Ḥasan-i-Ardakání, Ḥájí (Ḥájí Amín), 102n.
Abu'l-Ḥasan Khán (Aga Khan I), 21n.
Abu'l-Ḥasan Mírzá, Prince (Ḥájí Shaykhu'r-Ra'ís), 90 and n.
Abu'l-Qásim-i-Káshání, Áqá, 83
Abu'sh-Shurúr (Mírzá Asadu'lláh of Khuy), 43
Acre, *see* 'Akká
Ádharbáyján, 1, 67n.
Adrianople, 3, 47, 48, 64, 81, 82, 83, 120
Adventures of Hajji Baba of Ispahan, The, 22 and n.
Afghání, *see* Jamálu'd-Dín, Siyyid
Afghánistán, 23
Afnán, 52; *see* Báb, His family
Afnán-i-Kabír (the Great Afnán), *see* Ḥasan, Ḥájí Mírzá Siyyid
Aga Khan I, 21n.
Aḥmad, Ḥájí Mírzá, of Káshán, 64 and n.
Aḥmad, Tablets of (Persian and Arabic), 64 and n.
Aḥmad-i-Aḥsá'í, Shaykh, founder of Shaykhí sect, 15; mentioned, 20
Aḥmad-i-Kátib, Ḥájí Mírzá, 78, 80
Aḥmad-i-Rúḥí, Shaykh (Sheykh A—): correspondence with Browne, 18, 21, 72, 77; supplies Browne with *Hasht Bihisht*, 19–20; his character, 21; relation to Mírzá Áqá Khán, 21–3; chief translator of *Hajji Baba*, 22n.; meets Mírzá Yaḥyá and marries daughter, 23; supports Siyyid Jamálu'd-Dín, 26; imprisonment and death, 28; his part in authorship of *Hasht Bihisht*, 33, 72; slights *Nuqṭatu'l-Káf*, 72; mentioned, 72
Akhtar, 23
'Akká (Acre): Bahá'u'lláh's banishment to, and incarceration in, 5, 81; followers in, 82; murder of three Azalís, 34–7, 82; Browne's visit, 6, 48, 49–50, 52–4, 109, 118n., 122; Western Bahá'ís visit (1898–9), 115; 'Abdu'l-Bahá's confinement renewed (1902), 107–8; mentioned, 12, 22, 23, 28, 82, 83, 90n., 102n., 107, 110, 116, 120
'Aláu'l-Mulk, Persian Ambassador at Constantinople, 28
al-Azhar, Mosque and Theological College, 66, 107
Aleppo, 23
Alexandria, 64, 120n.
Alexandrine Tract, The, 65–6, 67
'Ali ibn Abí Ṭalib, son-in-law of Prophet Muḥammad, 41 and n.
'Alí Afnán, Ḥájí Siyyid ('Bábí agent at Beyrout'), conducts Browne to 'Akká, 52–4
'Alí-Akbar, Mírzá, cousin of Báb, 44
'Alí-Akbar, Siyyid, accuses Bahá'ís, 92
'Alí-Akbar Khán-i-Mílání, Mírzá, 35n.
'Alí-Akbar-i-Shahmírzádí, Ḥájí (Ḥájí Ákhund), Hand of the Cause, 102n.
'Alí Áqá, Mírzá, nationalist divine, 94
'Alí-Aṣghar Khán, Mírzá (the Amínu's Sulṭán), chief minister of Náṣiri'd-Dín Sháh, 25, 28, 29, 100
'Alí, Ḥájí Mírzá Siyyid, maternal uncle who reared the Báb, 12 and n., 42, 85
Ali-Kuli Khan (Nabíli'd-Dawlih), Persian Chargé d'Affaires, 93
''Alí, Mírzá'; father of author, 6; meetings with Browne, 12 and n.; correspondence with Browne, 6, 12, 14–17, 49–50, 61; his diary, 12; facilitates Browne's visit to Bahá'u'lláh, 6, 50, 52; Bahá'u'lláh refers to Browne's visit in Tablet, 52; Browne quotes letters on Bahá'í persecutions, 61; purchases *Táríkh-i-Jadíd* for Browne, 62
'Alí-Muḥammad, Mírzá (Varqá), poet, martyr, 30
'Alí-Muḥammad, Siyyid, *see* Báb, The
'Álí Páshá, Turkish Prime Minister, 15n., 64
'Alíy-i-'Arab, Siyyid, 33

Index

Bábíism, future of, 58, 61, 119; new spiritual force, 90

Bábís: persecution, 1, 7; at Badasht, 74–5; two attempt to assassinate Sháh, 1, 2, 44; slaughtered, 63 and n., 120; state after Báb's martyrdom, 42, 45; seek Bahá'u'lláh's return to Baghdád, 3, 78–9; condition then, 79; list of 'victims' eliminated by Bahá'ís, 82–3; author examines list, 83–4; Writings available to, 71; ignored *Nuqṭatu'l-Káf*, 72; most accept Bahá'u'lláh, 3, 72; some remain Baghdád, 81; opposed by Shaykhís, 15; Muslim accusations against, 75 and n.; doctrines, 74, 76; Browne's initial contacts with, 8–13; their spirit, 53, 118; Browne publishes 'The Bábís of Persia', 14; number and influence growing, 59; press accuses of assassinating Náṣiri'd-Dín Sháh, 30; none at Mírzá Yaḥyá's funeral, 112

Bábu'l-Báb, *see* Ḥusayn-i-Bushrú'í, Mullá

Bábulsar, 11

Badasht Conference, 74 and n., 75

Badí'u'lláh, Mírzá, son of Bahá'u'lláh, 99, 103

Badrí-Ján, wife of Mírzá Yaḥyá, 36, 37

Baghdád: Baghdád period, 2, 3, 44, 78–81, 83, 120; Bahá'u'lláh's Writings in, 12, 46; mentioned, 23, 47, 64

Bahá'í Proofs, The, 67

Bahá'í Revelation, The, 31n.

Bahá'í World, The (vol. IV), 110n.

Bahai'ism, new spiritual force, 90; success in America, 119; mentioned, 7, 88, 118, 119

Bahá'ís: opposed by Shaykhís, 15; four exiled to Cyprus, 82; pilgrims to 'Akká foiled, 36; seven murder Azalís in 'Akká, 36; Browne meets in Shíráz, 11–12, in Kirmán, 13, in Ṭihrán, 13–14; community after Bahá'u'lláh's ascension, 87; growth and influence, 88; suspected when Náṣiri 'd-Dín Sháh assassinated, 29; avoidance of Persian politics, 90–2; hostility of Shí'ah clergy, 91–2; their aims, 91–2, 100, 108; persecuted, 94–5, 99–103; their conduct, 100–1; American Bahá'ís, 115–16, 120, ethical teaching, 120, fraternity between races, 120; relation to Báb and disciples, 76

Bahá'u'lláh (Mírzá Ḥusayn 'Alí): titles, 'Glory of God', 1, 'He Whom God shall make manifest', 3, others given by Báb, 40; pilgrimage to 'Iráq, 42; response to attempt on Sháh's life (1852), 1–2, 44; imprisoned Síyáh-Chál, 2; realizes Divine Mission, 2; banished to 'Iráq, 2, 120; relation to Mírzá Yaḥyá, 3; withdraws for two years, 3, 43–4, 77–80; takes up Mission, 3; Bábís turn to, 71, 72, 81; attempt on life, 80–1; reveals *Kitáb-i-Íqán*, *Seven Valleys* and *Hidden Words*, 46 and n.1; removed to Constantinople, 3, 46 and n., 47; Declaration before going, 3, 46, 47; transferred to Adrianople, 3, 120; exiled to 'Akká, hardships, 4–5, 15n., 35, 64, 81–2, 120; sorrow at murder of three Azalís, 34, 36; addresses Ṭihrán, forecasts changes, 92–3; last years at Bahjí, 5; pitches tent on Mount Carmel, 5; receives Browne, 6, 12, 48, 53 and n.; Browne's pen-portrait of, 56–7, 122; Bahá'u'lláh mentions Browne in Tablet, frontispiece, 52; charges against in *Hasht Bihisht*, 33–4, 37; ascension, 22n., 103, 114, 120 and n.; Will and Testament, 86, 113; appoints 'Abdu'l-Bahá Successor, 113; Covenant broken, 86, 107, 113, 115; next Manifestation, 87; Writings: *Kitáb-i-Aqdas*, 66, 92–3, *see* Tablets, power of, 106, quotations from 2, 34, 77, 79, 92–3; followers

enjoined to eschew politics, 26; on newspapers, 31; inaccurate reports of scholars, 6–7; centenary of birth, 119; mentioned, 12, 22, 34n., 35n., 58 and n., 64, 66, 68 and n., 69, 70n., 72, 74n., 76, 80, 83, 88, 91n., 107, 115
Bahá'u'lláh, by H. M. Balyuzi, 44n., 63n., 83n.
Bahíyyih Khánum (Bahiyya Khánam), daughter of Bahá'u'lláh, 119 and n.
Bahjí, Mansion of, 5, 10n., 12, 53 and n., 56 and n., 118n.
Balkan Confederates, 97
Balyuzi, H. M.: father of, 6, and *see* "Alí, Mírzá'; see *Bahá'u'lláh*
Bardsír, 21 and n.
Barney, Laura Clifford, 116, 120
Barthold, Prof., Soviet orientalist, 67n.
Baṣír-i-Hindí, Siyyid, Indian Bábí, 43, 79
Baṣrah, 3
Bavánát, 9
Bayán (*Beyán*), *The:* major Writing of the Báb, 14n., 39n.; in British Museum, 14; part of Báb's title, 16 and n., 39 and n.; announces 'Him Whom God shall manifest', 39–40, 71, 84 and n.; mentioned, 20, 79, 112
Bayánís, 72
Beirut: 'Abdu'l-Bahá visits, 5; Browne travels to and from 'Akká from, 52, 54; mentioned, 16, 27n., 36, 114
Berlin, 100
Beyán, see *Bayán, The*
Bibliothèque Nationale, 63, 111
Blunt, Wilfrid Scawen, 24 and n.
Boer War, 106
Book of Certitude, The, see *Kitáb-i-Íqán*
Both Ends of the Candle, 13n., 21n., 60–1
Brief Narrative of Recent Events in Persia, A, 89
Brilliant Proof, The, 67 and n.
Britain, 120
British: Academy, Browne's paper to, 119; foreign policy, 24; Isles, first Bahá'í in, 110; Museum, 14, 41, 43n., 111; troops, 95
Brooklyn, N.Y., Miss A. H. of, 116
Browne, Sir Benjamin, father of E. G. Browne, 8
Browne, Edward Granville, M.A., M.B., F.B.A., F.R.C.P., Sir Thomas Adams' Professor of Arabic and Fellow of Pembroke College in the University of Cambridge: famed orientalist, 6; early life and studies, 8–10; encounters Bábí and Bahá'í Faith, 10; elected Fellow, 11; Reader in Persian, 13; visits Persia (1887–8), 11–13; elected to Royal Asiatic Society, 14; meets author's father, 12n., corresponds with him, 6, 12, 14–17, 49–50; works on Bábí and Bahá'í MSS., 14–15; publishes 'The Bábís of Persia' (1889), 14, 49 and n.; contacts Mírzá Yaḥyá and obtains copy of Báb's Tablet to, 37–9; sees original Tablet, 54; correspondence with Mírzá Yaḥyá, 18, 49, 54; corresponds with Shaykh Aḥmad-i-Rúhí, 18, 21, 22n., 49; his evaluation of, 21; receives *Hasht Bihisht*, 19–20; visits and describes Mírzá Yaḥyá (1890), 50–2, (1896), 39 and n. 3, 54; visits and describes Bahá'u'lláh (1890), 6, 12, 49–50, 52–4, 56–7; assisted by author's father, 6, 50, 52; Bahá'u'lláh refers to visit, frontispiece and 52; describes 'Abdu'l-Bahá, 57–8; MSS. given to Browne in 'Akká, 53–4; 'Abdu'l-Bahá on significance of visit, 104, 108; Shoghi Effendi on visit, 53n., 122; translates and edits *A Traveller's Narrative* (1891), 10 and nn., **55–61**; letter to 'Abdu'l-Bahá about, 55; *Oxford Magazine* attacks, 58–60; includes résumé of *Hasht Bihisht*, 33–4, 37; perpetuates errors, 80, 84; authorship, 72; meets Siyyid Jamá-

lu'd-Dín, 25, 28; publishes 'Catalogue and Description of 27 Bábí Manuscripts' (1892), 21; *A Year Amongst the Persians* published (1893), 6, 8 and n., 11, 13 and n., 14n., 15; translates and edits *Táríkh-i-Jadíd* (1893), 62; marks change his attitude, 62, 104; includes and evaluates Mírzá Yaḥyá's narrative, 41; Ḥájí Mírzá Jání's history, 65; compares Bahá'u'lláh and Mírzá Yaḥyá, 45, 49; compares doctrines of Báb and Bahá'u'lláh, 47–8; finds copy of *Nuqṭatu'l-Káf*, 63; authorship in doubt, 63–5, 88; gives résumé, 73; begins *Literary History of Persia* (4 vols., 1902–24), 22n., 46n., 89, 121; receives Persian Government document on Bahá'u'lláh from Nicolas, 46; his Introduction to *Abbas Effendi, His Life and Teachings* (1903), 58–60; support of Constitutional Movement: books written, other activities, 88, 89–90; Bahá'í persecutions unmentioned, 95; *Nuqṭatu'l-Káf* published (1910) with Browne's English and Persian Introductions, 70, 73, 88; his editorship denied, 74; attitude to, 85; wrong appraisal of, 88; meets 'Abdu'l-Bahá in London and Paris, 96–7, 110 and n., 111, 117; correspondence with 'Abdu'l-Bahá (1890–1913), 55, 96, **98–111**; corresponds with opponents of 'Abdu'l-Bahá, 96; publishes *Materials for the Study of the Bábí Religion (1918)*: contents discussed, **112-17**; mentions Faith to British Academy, 119; obituary of 'Abdu'l-Bahá, 119–21, 122; wife's death, 121; death, 121; a Persian obituary, 74; mistermed Bahá'ís as Bábís, 11, 31, 112, 118n.; perplexed by Mírzá Yaḥyá's defection, 48; estimate of Yaḥyá aids adversaries, 6; puzzled by 'Abdu'l-Bahá's station, 86–7; Ross regrets his Bábí studies, 60–1; his Bábí and Bahá'í documents at Cambridge University Library, 35n., 96, 98 and nn., 113; services to Bahá'í Faith, 6, 121–2

Budapest, 120

Buddha, 1

Bu<u>kh</u>ára, 66 and n.

Burhán-i-Lámi', see *Brilliant Proof, The*

Bushire (Bú<u>sh</u>ihr), 24

Bushrawayh, *see* Bu<u>sh</u>rúyih

Bu<u>sh</u>rúyih (Bushrawayh, Bushraweyh) 1, 75–6 and n.

Buṭrus al-Bustání, ed. *Dá'iratu'l-Ma'árif* (Arabic Encyclopaedia), 27 and n.

Buzurg-i-Núrí, Mírzá, father of Bahá'u'lláh, 1 and n.

Buzurg <u>Kh</u>án-i-Qazvíní, Mírzá (Persian Consul-general in Ba<u>gh</u>dád), 80

Byron, Lord, 24n.

Cairo, 29 and n., 66, 106, 107, 114, 115, 116

Calcutta, 22n., 24

Calligraphy, Persian styles, 14 and nn.

Cambridge: Browne in, 8, 9, 13, 54, 110, 113, 121; Pembroke College, vi, 5–6, 8, 11, 13, 55; University Library, vi, 10, 96, 98 and nn., 113; University Press, 112

Carmel, Mount, 115

Caspian Sea, 11

'Catalogue and Description of 27 Bábí Manuscripts', 19–20 and nn.

Chahár Maqála, 46n.

Chargé d'Affaires, Persian, in Washington, D.C., 93

Chicago, 114, 115, 120

<u>Ch</u>ihríq, 1

Christ (Jesus), 1, 50, 84, 104–5, 106, 109, 114; apostles of, 110

Christians, 103, 114

Churchill, Lord Randolph, 24

City Temple, London, 96

Index

Huseyn, Áká Mírzá Seyyed, *see* Muḥammad-Ḥusayn, Áqá Siyyid
Ibn Hishám, 71
Ibn Isḥáq (Ibn Is-ḥák), biographer of Prophet Muḥammad, 71 and n.
Ibn Ra<u>sh</u>íd, 24
Ibn Sa'úd, 24n.
Ibráhím-i-Ká<u>sh</u>í, Ḥájí, 83, 84
Ibráhím-i-<u>Kh</u>alíl, Siyyid, Bábí denounced by Mírzá Yaḥyá, 43
Imámate, 84–5
Imám-Jum'a (Imám-i-Jum'ih), of Famagusta, 112
India, 21n., 23, 24, 30n.–31n.
Indian Diary, An, 31n.
Írán (Persia): Government seeks Bahá'u'lláh's removal from Ba<u>gh</u>dád, 46–7; Browne's love for, 8, 10; Browne visits (1887–8), 11–13; effect of Bábí and Bahá'í Movements, 88; constitutional struggle, 89, 93; breakdown of law and order, 93–5, 97; foreign intervention, 93–6, 97; mentioned, 2, 13n., 19, 20, 25 and n., 27, 32, 83, 100, 101, 109
Iran (A Short Political Guide), 7n.
Iran, Past and Present, 7n.
Íràn<u>sh</u>ahr, 74
'Iráq, 2, 3, 26, 27, 42, 79
Ireland, 24n.
Isaiah xiv. 12, 112 and n.
Iṣfahán, 11, 12, 22, 34n., 50, 102 and n.
Ishmael, *see* Ismá'íl
'I<u>sh</u>qábád (Askabad), 66 and n.; Bahá'í House of Worship, 15n.
Islám, 1, 26, 60 and n., 66, 112
Ismá'íl, 64n.
Ismá'íl Pá<u>sh</u>á Ayyúb, Governor of Khartoum, 11
Ismá'íl-i-Qumí, Ḥájí Mullá, one of Seven Martyrs, 85
Ismá'íl-i-Ṣabbá<u>gh</u>-i-Sidihí, 35n.
Ismá'ílí sect, 21n.
Istanbul (Constantinople): Bahá'u'lláh in, 3, 47, 79, 83; Browne visits, 9, 21; <u>Sh</u>ay<u>kh</u> Aḥmad in, 18–20, 23; Siyyid Jamálu'd-Dín in, 25; mentioned, 4, 22n., 26, 28, 46, 104
Ithaca, N.Y., 115
I'timádu's-Salṭanih, Persian Minister of Publications, 24
Jackson, Stanley, 23n.
Jalálu'd-Dawlih, Governor of Yazd, 99, 102 and n.
Jamálu'd-Dín al-Af<u>gh</u>ání, Siyyid: birth and career, 23–4; contact with British statesmen, 24; meets Browne, 25; in Russia, 24–5; meets Náṣiri'd-Dín <u>Sh</u>áh and returns to Persia, 25; vendetta against <u>Sh</u>áh, 25–7; protagonist of Pan-Islamism, 23, 25–7; relation to <u>Sh</u>ay<u>kh</u> Aḥmad-i-Rúḥí and Mírzá Áqá <u>Kh</u>án, 26–8; engineers assassination of <u>Sh</u>áh, 28–9; called 'Babi leader', 31–2; Bahá'u'lláh mentions him, 27–8; hostility to Bahá'í Faith, 27–8, 108; conspires to embroil Bahá'ís in politics, 100–3
Ján, Mírzá Áqá (<u>Kh</u>ádimu'lláh) amanuensis of Bahá'u'lláh, 80
Jání, Ḥájí Mírzá, of Ká<u>sh</u>án, Bábí merchant and martyr: entertains the Báb, 63; writes brief history of Bábí Faith, 63, 65, 68, 69; *Táríkh-i-Jadíd* based on his work, 67, 68, 70 and n., 71; *Nuqṭatu'l-Káf* ascribed to him, 70n. 88; martyred, 71, 88; mentioned, 64, 84
Javád-i-Karbilá'í, Ḥájí Siyyid (Ḥájí Seyyed Jawád of Kerbelá): <u>Sh</u>í'ah divine who accepted Báb and Bahá'u'lláh, 68 and n., 80; authorship of *Ha<u>sh</u>t Bihi<u>sh</u>t* discussed, 20–1; mentioned, 78, 83–4
Jawád, Bábí woodcutter, 78
Jesus, *see* Christ
Jew, 3
Jináb-i-Bábu'l-Báb, 75
Journal of Royal Asiatic Society (J.R.A.S.), 14, 20 and n., 38 and n., 39n., 49 and n., 54nn.; Browne's obituary of 'Abdu'l-Bahá, 119–21

Judas Iscariot, 84
Kamshad, H., 7 and n., 22n.
Kansas City, 115
Karbilá (Kerbelá), 20 and n., 26, 68 and n., 78
Káshán, 63–5, 68, 69, 83
Kazemzadeh, Dr Firuz, 100n.
Káẓim-i-Rashtí, Siyyid, associate of Shaykh Aḥmad-i-Aḥsá'í, 15
Ḳazvín, *see* Qazvín
Kenosha, 115
Kerbelá, *see* Karbilá
Khabíru'l-Mulk, the, *see* Ḥasan Khán, Ḥájí Mírzá
Khádimu'lláh (Servant of God), 80
Khán 'Abdu'l-Qayyúm Khán, 60n.
Khartoum (Khartúm), 11 and n.
Khayru'lláh, Dr Ibráhím George, early Bahá'í teacher in America: account of, 114–16; his titles, 114; his teachings, 116; letter to Browne, 116; mentioned, 112
Khurásán, 1n., 95
Kirmán, 13, 14, 15, 21, 22, 95
Kitáb-i-Aqdas, 66, 91n., 92–3
Kitáb-i-Badáyiu'l-Áthár, diary of Mírzá Maḥmúd, 97n.
Kitáb-i-Íqán (The Book of Certitude), 12, 15n., 46 and n., 54, 67, 77 and n., 79
Kitáb-i-Nuqṭatu'l-Káf, **70–88**; Browne finds copy, 63; meaning of title, 72n.; authorship in doubt, 63–5, 70n., pronounced forgery by Mírzá Abu'l-Faḍl, 70, 72; Browne's editorship denied, 74; English and Persian Introductions, 70, 73–88; Browne's evaluation of, 70–1; résumé, 73; text confused, 73; reflects period of Bábí nihilism, 73; spelling inconsistency, 75–6; compared to *Táríkh-i-Jadíd*, 74–5, 81–2, 85–6; ignored by Bábís, 72; inconsistent with Azalí belief, 73; mentioned, 45, 116
Kitábu'l-Fará'id, 67
Krishna, 1
Kubíčková, Mme Věra, 7
Ḳum, *see* Qum
Kurdistán, 78, 80
Ḳurratu'l-Ayn, *see* Ṭáhirih
Lár, 94
Larnaca, 50
Lawḥ-i-'Álí Páshá, 15
Lawḥ-i-Burhán (Tablet of Proof), 15 and n.
Lawḥ-i-Malikih (Malika), Tablet to Queen Victoria, 14 and n.
Lawḥ-i-Sheykh Bákir, 15 and n.
Le Sage, author of *Gil Blas*, 22n.
Lebanon, 114
Letters of the Living, 33 and n., 42, 43, 51, 71n., 81 and n., 83
Levant, 114
Liberal Cabinet, in Britain, 90
Literary History of Persia, A, 22n., 89; refers to Bábí and Bahá'í Faith, 121; refers to Kitáb-i-Íqán, 46n.
London: Browne a student, 9, 12; Persia Committee, 89; 'Abdu'l-Bahá twice visits, 67n., 96, 110, 113, 117, 120; mentioned, 24, 100
'Lord of the Age', 51
Lucifer, 112
Lytton, Earl (4th) of, 24n.
Maḥbúbu'sh-Shuhadá, *see* Ḥusayn, Mírzá
Máh-kú, 1
Maḥmúd, Shaykh (the Afḍalu'l-Mulk), brother of Shaykh Aḥmad-i-Rúḥí, 22n.
Maḥmúd Páshá, Istanbul Police Chief, 28
Maḥmúd-i-Zarqání, Mírzá, secretary to 'Abdu'l-Bahá, 96, 97n.
Majlis, Persian National Assembly, 93; Parliament building bombarded, 95
Malkam (Malkom), Khán, Prince (the Náẓimu'd-Dawlih), Persian Minister in London (1872–89), ed. *Qánún*, 25 and n., 100 and n.; 'Abdu'l-Bahá mentions, 100, 101–2

Mánakjí, Zoroastrian agent, 67; encourages writings of *Táríkh-i-Jadíd*, 67–70, *passim*
Manifestations of God: preceding the Báb, 1; born in Ṭihrán, 93; after Bahá'u'lláh, 87; world's attitude toward, 47, 105, 109
Marlowe, John, 7 and n.
Mas͟hhad, 94
Mas͟hhad-i-Sar (Bábulsar), 11
Mas͟hriqu'l-Ad͟hkár, in 'Is͟hqábád, 66n.
Mas'úd Mírzá, Prince (the Ẓillu's-Sulṭán), eldest son of Náṣiri'd-Dín S͟háh, 102 and n.
Materials for the Study of the Bábí Religion: contents, **112–17**, 118–19; Browne on *Mustayqiẓ*, 43; Persian Foreign Minister demands Bahá'u'lláh's banishment, 46 and nn., 47 and n.; doctrines of Báb and Bahá'u'lláh, 47; Browne's last letter from Mírzá Yaḥyá, 54; lists 'Abdu'l-Bahá's Letters to Browne, 98 and n.; contains useful bibliography, 112; omits account of 'Abdu'l-Bahá's Western journey, 116; situation of Bahá'ís when written, 118–19; mentioned 34–5n., 107n., 120n.
Mázindarán, 94
Mecca, 23
Michigan, 114
Midḥat Pás͟há, Ottoman statesman, 5
Miftáḥu Bábi'l-Abwáb (The Key to the Gate of Gates), 29n., 107
Miftáḥu's-Salṭanih, Persian Consul-general, 31n.
Ministers: British in Persia, 24n.; Prime Ministers, Persian, 101 and *see* 'Alí-Aṣg͟har K͟hán, Mírzá and Áqásí, Ḥájí Mírzá; Prime Minister, Turkish, *see* 'Álí-Pás͟há; other Persian, of Interior, 95, in London, 25 and n., of Publications, 24
Minorsky, Prof. Vladimar, orientalist, 66n.
Mir'át (Mirror), 39n.
'Mírzá 'Alí,' *see* ''Alí, Mírzá'
Mírzáy-i-Hamadání, 102
Modern Iran, 7n.
Modern Persian Prose Literature, 7n., 22n.
Montagu, Edwin, 30n., 31n.
Montreal, 96n.
Morier, James, 22 and n.
'Morning (Morn) of Eternity', *see* Yaḥyá, Mírzá
Morning Post, 30, 32
Moses, 1, 109
'Most Great Peace', 53n., 57, 122
Mosul, 3
Muftí, of 'Akká, 5; Grand Muftí of Egypt, 5
Muḥammad, the Prophet of Islám, 1, 41n., 71, 109
Muḥammad 'Abduh, S͟hayk͟h, Grand Muftí of Egypt, 5
Muḥammad-'Alí, Mírzá, son of Bahá'u'lláh, 115; breaks His Covenant, 86; followers called 'Unitarians', 86
Muḥammad-'Alí K͟hán, Bahá'í of Ṭihrán, 95
Muḥammad-'Alí S͟háh (reigned 1907–9); as Crown Prince executes S͟hayk͟h Aḥmad-i-Rúhí and Mírzá Áqá K͟hán, 28; *coup d'état*, 89, 93; deposed, 89 and n., 93; attempts to regain throne, 93; mentioned, 95
Muḥammad-'Alíy-i-Bárfurús͟hí (Quddús), last Letter of the Living, 33n., 42, 51, 71, 73, 74n., 75, 81 and n.
Muḥammad-'Alíy-i-Zanjání, Mullá (Ḥujjat), outstanding Bábí, 42, 73
Muḥammad-Báqir, Mírzá, of Bavánát (Káfir, Mu'aṭṭar): background, 9, Persian tutor to Browne, 9; author, 9; in Ṭihrán, 16
Muḥammad-Báqir, S͟hayk͟h (D͟hi'b, the Wolf), divine of Iṣfahán and persecutor of Bahá'ís, 15n.
Muḥammad, Ḥájí Siyyid, the Báb's

maternal uncle; *Kitáb-i-Íqán* revealed for, 12 and n.
Muḥammad ibn-i-Ḥasan al 'Askarí, twelfth Imám, 84–5
Muḥammad-Ḥusayn, Áqá Siyyid (Áká Mírzá Seyyed Huseyn), nephew of Báb's wife and grandfather of Shoghi Effendi, 14 and n.
Muḥammad-i-Iṣfahání, Siyyid, 'Antichrist of the Bahá'í Revelation', 3, 34 and n., 36, 37, 78, 79, 80, 82, 83
Muḥammad-Ismá'íl, Ḥájí (Dhabíh), of Káshán, 64 and n.
Muḥammad-Ja'far, Mullá (the Shaykhu'l-'ulamá), of Kirmán, father of Shaykh Aḥmad-i-Rúḥí, 21
Muḥammad-Ja'far-i-Naráqí, Mullá, 'Witness of the Bayán', 78–80 *passim*
Muḥammad Javád (Jawád), Mírzá, of Qazvín (Qazwín), his account of Bábí and Bahá'í history, 112–13, 115
Muḥammad-Karím Khán-i-Kirmání, Ḥájí, leader of Shaykhís, 15, 23
Muḥammad Khán, Ḥájí, leader of Shaykhís, 23
Muḥammad Khán-i-Qazvíní, Mírzá, critic and bibliographer; writes obituary of Browne, 74
Muḥammad-i-Mázindarání, servant of Mírzá Yaḥyá, 44
Muḥammad-Mihdí Khán, Dr Mírzá (Za'imu'd-Dawlih): ed. *Hikmat*, 29n.; author of refutation of Bábí and Bahá'í Faith, 29n., 107, 109; Browne evaluates, 107; 'Abdu'l-Bahá replies to, sends copy to Browne, 108–9; mentioned, 29
Muḥammad-Riḍá, Ḥájí Mírzá: Browne mentions, author queries identity, 78, 80
Muḥammad-Riḍáy-i-Kirmání, Mírzá, assassinates Náṣiri'd-Dín Sháh, 27, 28–9
Muḥammad Sháh, 34n., 42
Muḥammad-Taqí, Ḥájí Mírzá (Ḥájí Vakílu'd-Dawlih), cousin of the Báb, and chief builder of first Mashriqu'l-Adhkár, 15 and n.
Muḥammad-Taqí, Mullá, a 'Witness of the Bayán', 79
Muḥammad-i-Zarandí, Mullá (Nabíl-i-A'ẓam), historian of Ministries of Báb and Bahá'u'lláh, 44, 76; mentioned 14, 113 and n.
Muḥibu's-Sulṭán, 35n.
Mujtahid, 91n.
Mullás, 90 and n.
Munich, 23, 25
Músá, Mírzá (Kálim), faithful brother of Bahá'u'lláh, 78–9
Músáy-i-Qumí, Ḥájí Mírzá, learned divine, 79
Mushíru'd-Dawlih, *see* Ḥusayn Khán, Ḥájí Mírzá
Mushíru't-Tujjár, Bahá'í of Sárí, 94
Muslims, 25, 26, 91
Muṣṭafá, Mírzá (Ismá'íl-i-Ṣabbágh-i-Sidihí), supplied documents to Browne, 35n.
Mustayqiẓ (Sleeper Awakened), 43 and n., 44
Mu'taminu'l-Mulk, *see* Sa'íd Khán, Mírzá
Mutanabbi, al-, Arab poet, 21 and n.
Muẓaffari'd-Dín Sháh (reigned 1896–1907), 29, 102n.
'Mystic Source', 77–8, 79
Nabíl, numerical value, 38n.
Nabíl's Narrative see *The Dawn-Breakers*
Nabíl-i-A'ẓam, *see* Muḥammad-i-Zarandí, Mullá
Nabíli'd-Dawlih, *see* Ali-Kuli Khan
Najaf, 26
Námiy-i-Bástán, 26 and n., 27
Napoleon III, 14 and n.
Násikhu't-Tawáríkh (*Násikhu't-Taváríkh*), 68 and n.
Náṣir, the 'Arab, 34n.
Náṣiri 'd-Dín Sháh (reigned 1848–96): attempt on life (1852), 1, 36, 44, 63

and n.; Government seeks Bahá'u'lláh's removal from Baghdád, 46–7, 81; Bahá'u'lláh's Tablet to, 54; meets Siyyid Jamálu'd-Dín, 23, 25; jubilee celebration, 28; assassination, 27, 28–9; persecution of Bahá'ís, 29–30; British press reaction, 30–2 *passim*; mentioned, 3, 34n. 68 and nn. 81n., 100
Naskh, style of calligraphy, 14 and n.
Naṣru'lláh, Mírzá, brother-in-law of Mírzá Yaḥyá, 36
Nayríz, 94–5
Náẓimu'd-Dawlih, *see* Malkam Khán, Prince
New History of the Báb, see *Táríkh-i-Jadíd*
New York, 113, 114, 115, 120
Newcastle-on-Tyne, 8, 121
Newspapers, *see* Periodicals; see *The Times*, also press reports; Bahá'u'lláh counsels, 31
Nicolas, A.-L.-M., 46 and n., 81
Níyávarán, 1
Nuqṭatu'l-Káf, see *Kitáb-i-Nuqṭatu'l-Káf*
Nuqṭiy-i-Bayán, Ḥaḍrat, *see* Báb, The
Ottoman Government, 81, 82, 107
Oxford, 60
Oxford Magazine, The, 58–60 and n.
Pan-Islamic movement, 25, 27; 'Protagonist of Pan-Islamism', 23
Pantheism, 73
Paris, 24, 96, 97, 102n., 110n., 115, 117, 120
Pembroke College, Cambridge, vi, 5, 8, 11, 13
Periodicals, Foreign: *Akhtar*, 23; *Ḥablu'l-Matín*, 91; *Ḥikmat*, 29n.; *Íránshahr*, 74; *Qánún*, 25n., 100, 101; *Urwathu'l-Wuthqá*, 24; *Zapiski*, 66n.
Persia, *see* Írán
Persia and the Persian Question, 30 and n.
Persia Committee, 89
Persian Constitutional Movement, The, 119n.
Persian Crisis of December 1911, The, 89
Persian Literature in Modern Times, 89n.
Persian Revolution of 1905–1909, The, 25 and n., 27n., 28 and n., 29 and n., 89; Browne on Bahá'í attitude toward Persian politics, 90–1, 92; 'Abdu'l-Bahá on Persian constitutional struggle and foreign intervention, 95–6; mentioned, 91n.
Phelps, Myron H., 58, 60n., 73n., 113, 119, 120
Philadelphia, 115
Phillott, Col. D. C., 22n., 32
Pioneer, The, 30
Plevna, 8
Pontiff, 45, 47
Port Said, 120n.
Postal service, 94
Press and Poetry of Modern Persia, The, 74 and n., 89
Press reports, 6, 30, 32
'Primal Point', *see* Báb, The
Qahír, *see* Rajab-'Alíy-i-Qahír, Mullá
Qá'im, the Promised One of Islám, 1, 15, 40 and n.
Qájár dynasty, 26, 43, 92, 99
Qánún, 25n., 100, 101
Qavámu'l-Mulk, grandee of Shíráz, 94
Qayyúm, 60n.
Qazvín (Ḳazvín), 42, 71, 102n.
Quddús, *see* Muḥammad-'Alíy-i-Bárfurúshí
Qum, 50n., 78 and n., 80 and n.
Qur'án, 64n.
Qurratu'l-'Ayn, *see* Ṭáhirih
Ra'ísu'l-Ḥukamá, 29n.
Rajab-'Alíy-i-Qahír, Mullá, 33, 34n., 35n., 78, 80
Rashídu's-Sulṭán, partisan of Sháh, 95
Rasht, 22, 91
Rawẓatu's-Ṣafá (*Rawḍatu's-Ṣafá*), 68 and n.

Index

Sírján (Kirmán province), 95
Síyáh-Chál, prison, 2
Some Answered Questions, 116
Spectator, The, 30
State Department, American, 93
Stuttgart, 120
Ṣubḥ-i-Azal, *see* Yaḥyá, Mírzá
Sublime Porte, The (Báb-i-'Álí), 4 and n., 28 and n.
Súdán, 11n.
Ṣúfí, 10
Sulaymáníyyih, 78
Sulṭán, Shaykh, accompanies Bahá'u'lláh from Kurdistán, 78, 79, 80
Sulṭánu'sh-Shuhadá, *see* Ḥasan, Mírzá
Sun of Truth, *see* Manifestations of God
Sunní, 25, 27, 74
Ṣúriy-i-Ra'ís, Tablet of Bahá'u'lláh, 64
Syria, 109, 120
Syrian Protestant College, 114
Ṭabarsí, Shaykh (Sheykh), fortress and shrine, 80n., 81 and n., 118
Tablets, of Bahá'u'lláh: Aḥmad, 64 and n.; *Alwáḥ*, 14; to Khayru'lláh, 114; *Súriy-i-Ra'ís* (to 'Álí Páshá), 64; *Lawḥ-i-Malikih* (to Queen Victoria), 14 and n.; to Náṣiri'd-Dín Sháh, 54; *Ṭarázát*, 31; *of the World*, 27, 102n.; *see* listings under *Lawḥ*; of 'Abdu'l-Bahá: 'Seven Candles of Unity', 110; to Hands of the Cause, 65; on Bahá'ís and politics, 91–2 and n.; on foreign intervention in Írán, 95–6; to Browne, 96, ch. IX
Tabríz, 1, 10 and n., 28, 29, 85, 94, 107
Ṭáhirih (Qurratu'l-'Ayn), Letter of the Living, martyr, poet, 42, 71 and n.; discards veil at Badasht, 74n., mentioned, 51, 73, 78
Táríkh-i-Jadíd (New History of the Báb), **ch. VII**; Browne translates and edits, 62; author, 62, 65; circumstances of composition, 65, 68–70; no copies reliable, 69; date composed, 72 and n.; Ḥájí Mírzá Jání's history, 65 and n., 70–1 and nn.; Introduction influenced by Azalís, 104; facsimile and translation of Báb's Tablet to Mírzá Yaḥyá, 38 and n.; Mírzá Yaḥyá's narrative, 41; compares Bahá'u'lláh and Mírzá Yaḥyá, 45 and n., 49; compares doctrines of Báb and Bahá'u'lláh, 47 and n.; résumé of *Nuqṭatu'l-Káf*, 70 and n., 71, 73; comparisons to *Nuqṭatu'l-Káf*, 74–5, 81–2, 85; Browne's attitude to, 85; mentioned, 49, 67, 76nn., 104
Teheran, *see* Ṭihrán
Thiqatu'l-Islám, 94
Thornburgh-Cropper, Mrs 110
Tiberias, 105
Tiflís (Tbilsi), 67 and n.
Ṭihrán (Teheran): Bahá'u'lláh imprisoned, 2; Seven Martyrs, 85–6; Bahá'u'lláh addresses, 92–3; Browne visits, 13, 50; Sháh assassinated, 29; *coup d'état* of 1908, 93; mentioned, 1, 16, 22, 24, 36, 46, 67, 69 and n., 78, 91n., 92, 94, 95, 102n., 114
Times, The, 30, 100
Toumansky, Alexander G., 66 and n.3; wife, 67n.
Traveller's Narrative, A, **55–61**; Browne encounters Faith, 10 and n.; Capt. Young's visit to Mírzá Yaḥyá, 37–8 and nn.; Browne receives copy in 'Akká, 54; evaluates significance, 55; author was 'Abdu'l-Bahá, 55; Browne describes Mírzá Yaḥyá, 51–2 and nn.; Browne at Bahjí, 53 and nn.; describes and quotes Bahá'u'lláh, 56–7; describes 'Abdu'l-Bahá, 57–8; résumé of *Hasht Bihisht*, 33–4 and n., 37; *Oxford Magazine* review, 58–60; mentioned, 12 and n., 45n., 48n., 53, 54, 58, 83, 118
Treasurer-general, *see* Shuster, W. Morgan
Trebizond, 28